Building the Weekend Skiff

by Richard Butz & John Montague

Text by Richard Butz
Illustrations by John Montague

TILLER
PUBLISHING
St. Michaels, MD

Published 1997 in the United States by Tiller Publishing, P.O. Box 447, St. Michaels, MD, USA .

ISBN 1-888671-10-6

Questions regarding the contents of this book should be addressed to:
    Tiller Publishing
    P.O. Box 447
    St. Michaels, MD 21663
    1-410-745-3750 Fax 1-410-745-9743

Cover photographs by Richard Butz & John Montague.
Front cover: Hannah Butz, the author's daughter, and Clancy enjoy The Weekend Skiff.
Back cover: Author Butz demonstrates variations of the Skiff.

Graphic design by Words & Pictures, Inc., 27 South River Road South, Edgewater, MD, 21037.

Printed in the USA by McNaughton & Gunn, 960 Woodland Drive, Saline, MI 48176.

Table of Contents

INTRODUCTION

The Name

We considered a variety of names for this boat: the Buffalo Skiff; the Bird Island Skiff; the Four Panel Boat; the Week-End Skiff. Each had its own rationale.

The Buffalo Skiff had great appeal because the boat was designed in Buffalo, a city that is rediscovering its waterfront. But John Montague, who adapted the first prototype and who launched the boat at Bird Island, in the Niagara River and Black Rock Canal, felt an attachment to that site and name. Since he built the first skiff it seemed right that he should name it the Bird Island Skiff.

The Four Panel Boat suggests that you can build the boat with four sheets of plywood. So what? The materials cost for this skiff is so meager that we didn't think prospective builders would be swayed by the amount of plywood consumed. After all, it's the labor that really matters: that sweat and blood that bonds the builder to the boat.

The Week-end Skiff suggests that you can build the boat in a week-end which is certainly true. But my wife, who fielded many calls regarding the Six-Hour Canoe, cautioned us against using a title with a time connotation in it. Yes, it is possible to build the Six-Hour Canoe in six hours, but most take longer and the title can create the impression that one is a bit slow if he or she doesn't finish in six hours. And, while we routinely build the skiff in a week-end, most people would want to take longer to do a good job. But our publisher weighed in, suggesting that a name that connected the boat to the Six-Hour Canoe and its simple construction would attract prospective builders and book buyers. So, confronted with that inescapable logic, the choice became obvious.

The Design Philosophy

As educators, John and I are interested in the process and what it can do for people. Our book, **Building The Six-Hour Canoe,** opened the doors to thousands of first-time builders, building their confidence and self-esteem as they built the boat. It also convinced many teachers and community leaders that they could build boats with kids in school, community and scouting programs and use the process to build positive values and to facilitate communication between adults and kids.

After publication of the book and an article in *WoodenBoat Magazine*, we received hundreds of calls concerning the plans and video for the canoe. Many times we were asked if we had plans for a simply built boat that could hold more than one adult. So many, in fact, that we were motivated to get busy and design just such a boat.

The design parameters were evident from the beginning: an eye catching skiff that could be built at low cost with basic hand tools. It should be adaptable for oars, sail or a small electric or gasoline outboard motor.

To begin the process, John started with a Six-Hour Canoe and simply expanded its beam and added a transom. Several years ago a student of mine built a canoe that was about four inches wider than originally planned and the resulting increase in stability and buoyancy was significant. But the addition of the transom and a foot of beam made an even bigger difference. And, it really looked salty.

John added fixed seats and oar locks and we put the boat through sea trials in the midst of a snow storm (this is Buffalo). We then tried some different transom designs, a sailing rig and built about ten more skiffs with students and kids in community and church programs to work out the bugs.

The result is the Week-End Skiff.

Some Advice on Building For Novice or First-Time Builders

This is a very straightforward boat to build. Read this manual through to get a sense of the process, but don't get bogged down on the details. Let the details become evident as you build - there's a logic to them that will carry you through.

Assemble your tools and materials so you won't need to stop and run out to the store every time you start a new section. Be sure your tools are sharp and properly adjusted. And be sure you know how to use them safely. And remember, although hand tools are slower than power tools, they don't get you into trouble as fast.

If a process is unfamiliar, work it out on pieces of scrap until you get the hang of it. I often make test cuts or patterns out of scrap to be sure what I'm doing is going to work out. You may even discover a better way to do the job in the process.

Try to interest a friend or family member in the project. An extra set of hands is necessary as you put the boat together. And an extra brain is sometimes helpful as you try to figure out how to do something.

So. get your tools and materials together and get to work. In no time you'll be fishing or messing around in a boat you built yourself.

Good luck!

USING THIS MANUAL

The primary thrust of this manual is the construction of a fifteen foot rowing skiff and the chapters are laid out to take you through the building of that boat. However, at the end of the manual are chapters detailing options for an outboard version accommodating a small motor and also for a sailing version.

The manual is organized in a linear format following the steps in building the rowing skiff. When we arrive at a point where you would do something differently for one of the other boats I'll alert you so you can refer to the appropriate section for guidance.

I would urge you to read through the entire manual before beginning construction. When I built my first boat, a Mirror Dinghy, I studied the manuals thoroughly so I would know what I was getting into — and it helped. And I really *hate* reading directions.

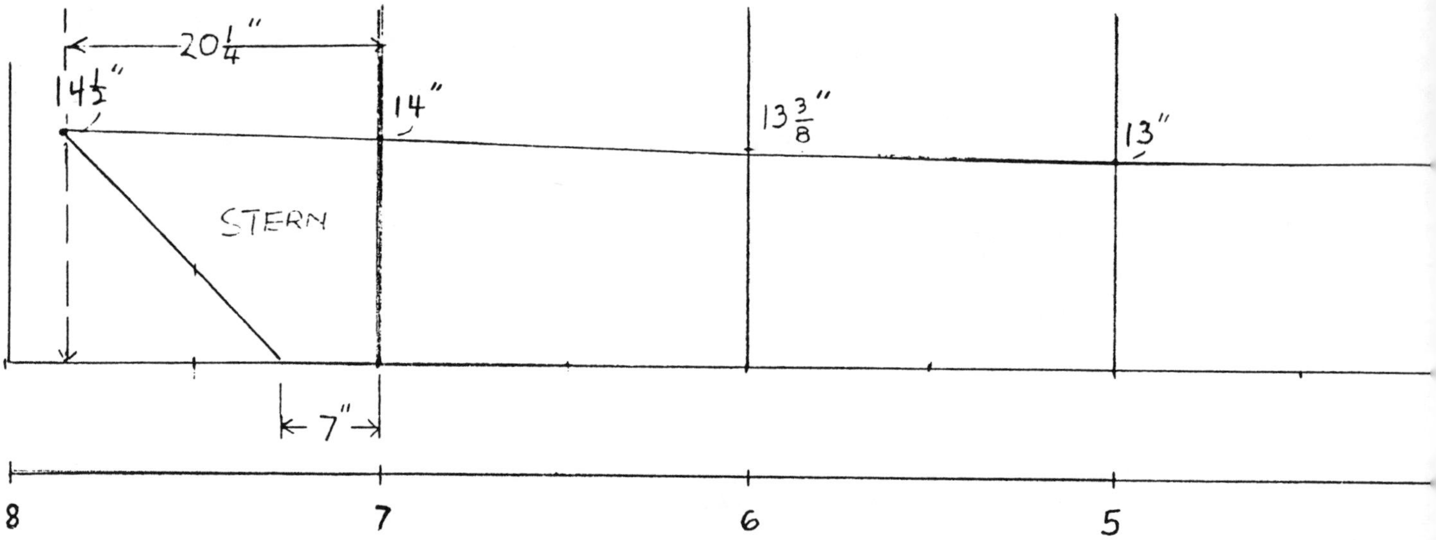
20 1/4"
14 1/2"
14"
13 3/8"
13"
STERN
7"
8
7
6
5

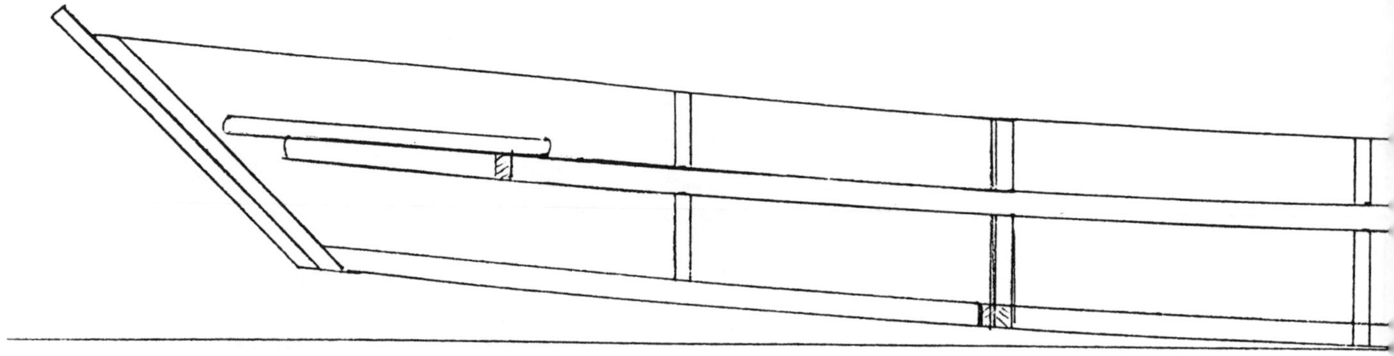

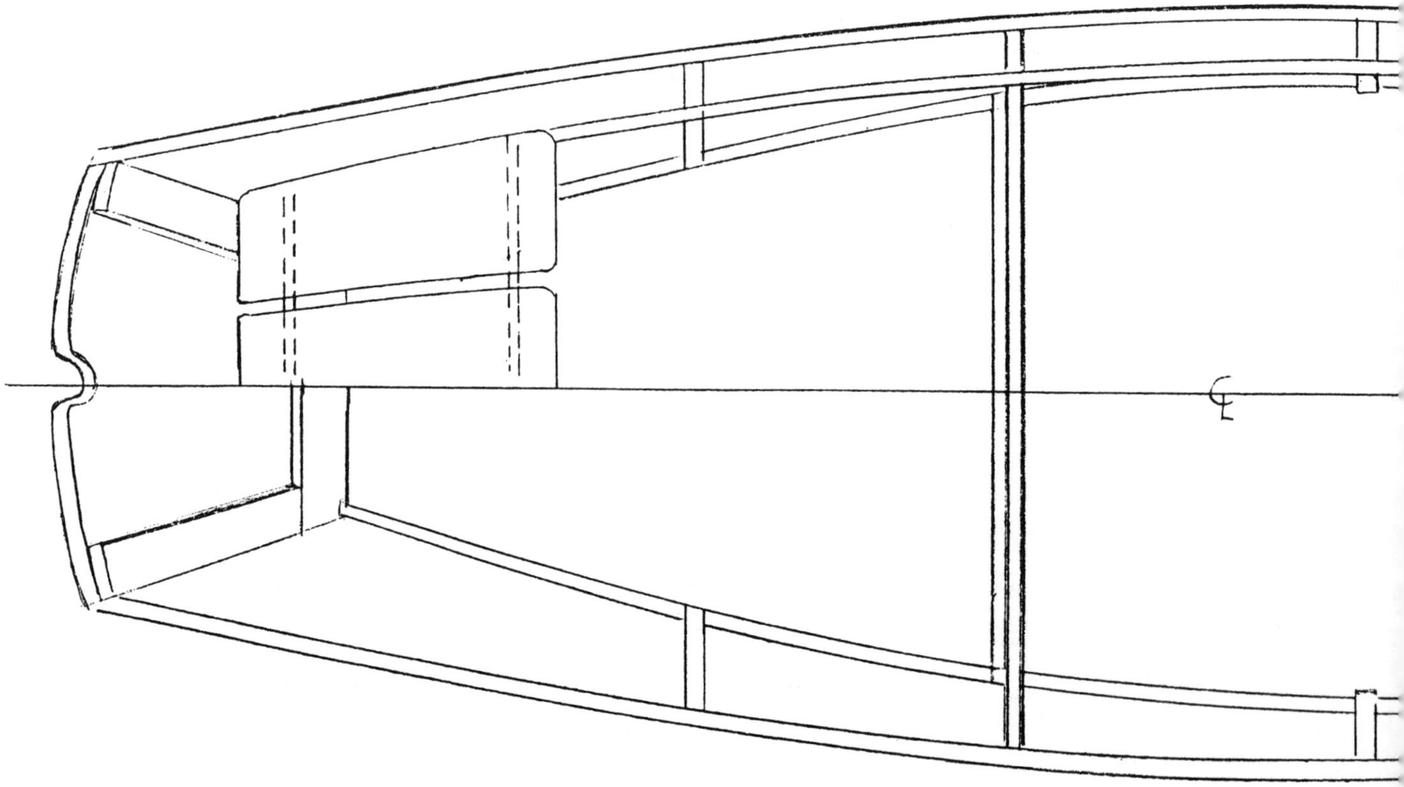
℄

$13\frac{1}{2}$

$14\frac{1}{2}''$

$16''$

$17\frac{1}{2}''$

BOW

$1''$

18"

PANEL LAYOUT

3   2   1   0

SCALE IN FEET

0 3 6 9 12   2   3   4

SECTION I —
PREPARATION

Part I: Materials

This is a plywood boat with dimensional lumber parts. It is glued, nailed and screwed together.

You can use first rate materials or you can use an economy grade - the differences will be in appearance and longevity. I prefer to use good quality native lumber, stainless steel fastenings and serviceable paints and varnishes for a job that both looks good and will last longer with proper care. So that's what I'll specify, but you can make your own choices.

You can also sheathe the boat with fiberglass, an expensive and time consuming process. I don't think it is necessary, but, if you want the boat to last for a very long time, and intend to give it hard use, you can do it and I'll give you some instruction in the process under the section on finishing.

Plywood

You can use regular exterior grade plywood if you choose or if marine plywood is not easily available. However marine grade plywood is sanded on both sides and has fewer voids than exterior grade so you get a better surface out of it and will have less risk of it collapsing if you bend it over a void.

#	dimension & description:	used for:
2 sheets	1/4" x 4' x 8' fir marine plywood	side panel
2 sheets	3/8" x 4' x 8' fir marine plywood	bottom and transom
1/2 sheet	1/2" x 4' x 8' fir marine plywood	rudder and centerboard for the sailing skiff

Dimensional Lumber

The lumber listed below is available at most lumber yards. It may not be the most economical way to purchase stock, but I am assuming that you don't have access to a table saw. If you do, you can save money by buying right and ripping out the sizes you need. For example: I often find fairly clear common pine or decking cedar in 1 x 6 sizes and rip out the 1 x 1 1/2 stock that I need for less money than if I bought 1 x 2.

You can also substitute. I've successfully used white pine. sugar pine, yellow pine, western red cedar, juniper, spruce and fir. I prefer softwoods because they tend to be lighter than hardwoods and they take fastenings - particularly ring nails - more easily.

1 pc.	1" x 1" x 16'	clear, straight pine	(batten for laying out lines, then use it for a keel)
1 pc.	2" x 4" x 3'	spruce, pine or fir	(stem)
1 pc.	1" x 2" x 16'	pine or fir	(frames)

Because the following pieces will be bent around or within the curve of the boat they should be relatively free of large knots.

2 pcs.	1" x 2" x 16'	pine or fir	(chine logs and half frames)
2 pcs.	1" x 2" x 16'	pine or fir	(gunwales)
2 pcs.	1" x 2" x 16'	pine or fir	(seat risers)

The following pieces may contain knots since they do not have to bend.

1 pc.	1" x 4" x 8'	pine or fir	(transom battens)
1 pc.	1" x 4" x 14'	pine or fir	(keelson for sailing skiff)
1 pc.	1" x 10" x 14'	pine or fir	(seats)

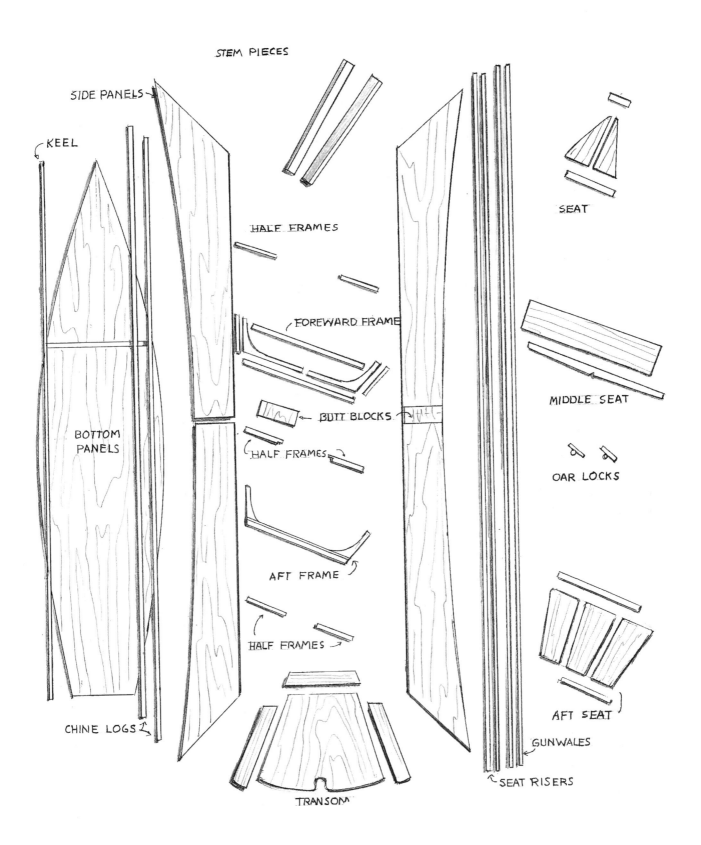

STEM PIECES

SIDE PANELS

KEEL

HALF FRAMES

FOREWARD FRAME

BUTT BLOCKS

HALF FRAMES

BOTTOM PANELS

AFT FRAME

HALF FRAMES

CHINE LOGS

TRANSOM

SEAT

MIDDLE SEAT

OAR LOCKS

AFT SEAT

GUNWALES

SEAT RISERS

Note: stock sizes are listed — actual dimensions are smaller. For example: 2" x 4" is actually 1 5/8" x 3 1/2" and 1" x 2" is actually 3/4" x 1 1/2", etc. If you are ripping out your own stock you can use either the size listed or reduce the dimensions to duplicate what you'd get at the lumber yard.

Fastenings

1 lb.	1" bronze ring nails	(stem, transom, chine logs, bottom)
50	# 8 x 3/4" stainless flat head screws	(gunwales, seat risers)
50 - 60	# 8 x 1 1/4" stainless flat head screws	(gunwales, seats)

Note: you can also use bronze fastenings, but they are softer and harder to drive. If the boat is going to be used in salt water, however, I would use silicon bronze to reduce reaction with the bronze ring nails. You could also put the boat together with galvanized fastenings.

1 lb	#8 x 1" drywall screws	(temporary fastenings)
1 qt.*	two part epoxy and pumps	will need more if you glass the hull - at least a gallon
2lb. bag	wood flour or Cabosil	
24"	4" fiberglass tape - 6 ounce	backing for the butt blocks
19'	6 ounce fiberglass cloth 60" wide	*optional*: for fiber glassing the hull

Miscellaneous

1 pr.	oar locks
1 set	7' oars
3 qts.	marine primer (optional, see finishing section)
1 pt.	marine varnish
1 gal.	paint (marine or latex exterior house paint (see finishing section)
amt.?	#'s 80 and 120 sandpaper
amt.?	# 220 wet sandpaper
1 sht.	# 50 sandpaper from a floor sander
roll	duct tape
sheet	plastic drop cloth
tube	contact cement for the sanding board
pint	ammonia for cleaning off the epoxy blush

Part II: Tools

Necessary

- sliding t-bevel
- combination square
- 16' tape measure
- 4' straight-edge
- sharp cross-cut hand saw
- sharp low angle block plane
- 3/8" electric drill, preferably variable speed and, even better, cordless. (Generally, cordless drills are more sensitive when driving screws into wood)
- #'s 2 and 3 Phillips head bits

- 1/16", 1/8" and 3/8" drill bits
- screw driver - Phillips and regular
- # 6-8 counter-sink bit
- electric saber saw and wood cutting blades
- hammer
- 2 12" - 18" or larger bar clamps
- 2 3" C-clamps
- 8 2" spring clamps
- set of saw horses - at least 36" wide
- 2 dozen acid brushes for glue application
- 2 dozen 6 ounce paper cups for glue mixing
- pencils

Optional

- band saw - particularly useful for cutting gussets and the stem
- table saw - useful for ripping stock to size
- random orbit sander - a great tool for efficient sanding of all parts of the boat

Essential

A builder's chair is necessary for sitting in when you are trying to solve a problem and for relaxing in at the end of the day when you just want to appreciate what you've accomplished. It is also a good place to "park" observers so they stay out of your way — and you will have observers.

Speaking of observers: we've found that the "Tom Sawyer Effect" applies in boat building. It looks like so much fun, and people are so engaged by it that we never have any problem enlisting help when we need it. You'll probably find this to be the case, too.

SECTION II —
CONSTRUCTION AND FINISHING

Part I: Making the Parts

A. Epoxy

Critical to this project is the proper preparation of epoxy. Read the instructions for whatever brand you are using - they are each unique products — and follow them closely. We recommend epoxy because it is strong, durable, clear and water resistant. It can also be used as a base for fillers such as wood flower and silica. When using the epoxy always liberally coat both faces to be joined and clamp lightly or fasten with nails or screws as indicated. And, always wipe off any excess so you don't have to sand it off later.

During some of the gluing operations, the process calls for thickened epoxy. To thicken the epoxy mix the epoxy thoroughly and then add wood flour or a filler such as Cabosil until the mixture has the consistency of peanut butter. It should always be applied after the gluing surface has been "wetted out" with unthickened epoxy.

You should also be aware that, upon curing, epoxy develops an amine "blush", a wax like substance that must be washed off with solvent or ammonia and water before recoating. Failure to do this may result in poor bonding of subsequent coats. The exception to this rule is that if you recoat before the epoxy sets, that is, while it is still tacky, you can avoid having to wash off the amine as it has not yet formed.

Finally, uncured epoxy comes off your hands with citrus based hand soaps that are now widely available.

B. Constructing the Stem

1. The stem is made from a 36" piece of 2" x 4". First cut a 36" piece from one of your 2 x 4's. Then tilt the band saw table 28° and make diagonal cut along the length of the 2 x 4 so you end up with two equal pieces.

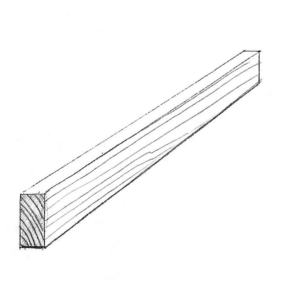

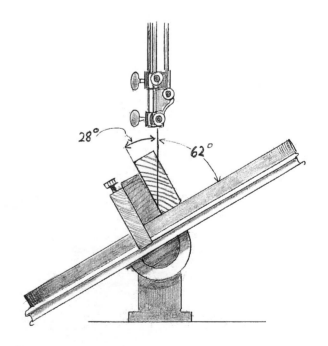

2. Apply a liberal dose of epoxy to the sawn faces of the 2 x 4. Then, immediately, apply a second coat of epoxy thickened with wood flour and clamp the two halves together as shown in the drawing. (*See page* 13.)

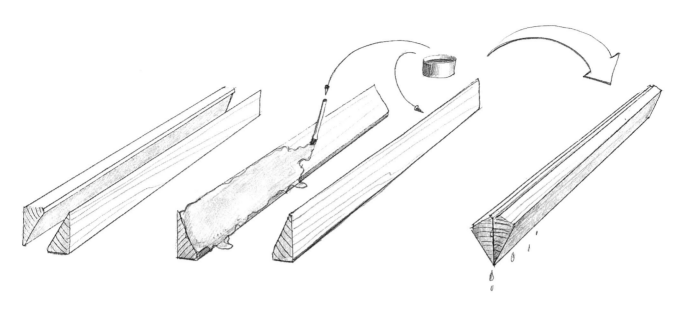

C. Hull panels (sides)

1. Lay two 1/4" x 4' x 8' pieces of plywood end-to-end on the floor. Be sure the ends are butted together tightly (you could temporarily duct tape them together). Using the plans as a reference, divide the plywood into 2' segments (called stations) and draw lines across the panels as shown (making station lines). Mark one end the bow and the other the stern. (*See layout illustration on page* 14.)

Transfer the measurements from the plans to the plywood by marking points on the station lines as measured from the two longitudinal edges of the plywood. These points will locate the sheer line (top edge) for each hull side panel. Drive a finishing nail into each point to serve as a guide for the batten.

When all the points have been marked spring your batten (the 1" x 1" x 16' piece of clear stock) against the points and then draw your sheer lines for each hull side panel.

Again, referring to the plans, locate the points for the bow and stern angles and draw them on the plywood. **Note: If you are building the outboard version refer to that section and mark the stern angle accordingly as the outboard transom is more vertical than the skiff.**

Again, referring to the plans, locate the position of the frames and half-frames and mark these on the panels. Note that these members are perpendicular to the bottom (straight) edges of the hull panels.

Now, step back and inspect what you've done. Be sure it matches the plans.

2. Remove the duct tape and carefully cut out the two side hull sections with a saber saw leaving the line for reference. Clamp the two sides of the bow section together and plane the edges smooth and to the line. Do the same with the stern sections.

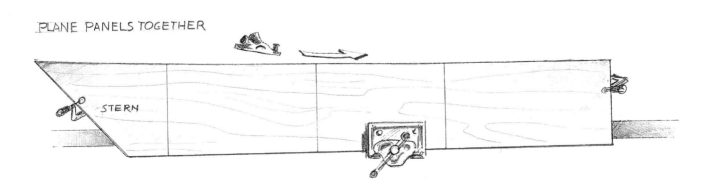

PLANE PANELS TOGETHER

STERN

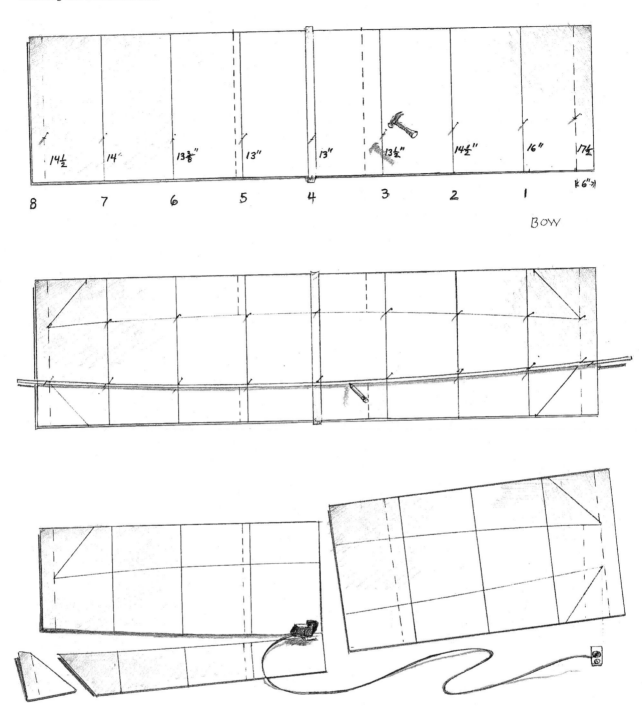

3. Using some scrap 1/4" plywood, cut two butt blocks, each 4" x 12".

4. Lay the panel sections out on the floor so the bottom edges of each side are opposite each other. The sides that are facing up will now become the insides of the boat. Mark them as such. Stretch a line from one end of the boat to the other along the straight edges (bottom) of the hull section and adjust to insure that they are straight. Center the butt blocks over the joints with their bottom edges 1 1/2" up from the bottom edges of the hull panels and draw a pencil line around them to mark where you will apply the epoxy (glue lines). The 1 1/2" gaps from the bottom are to allow for the positioning of the chine logs when they are installed later. (*See illustrations page* 15).

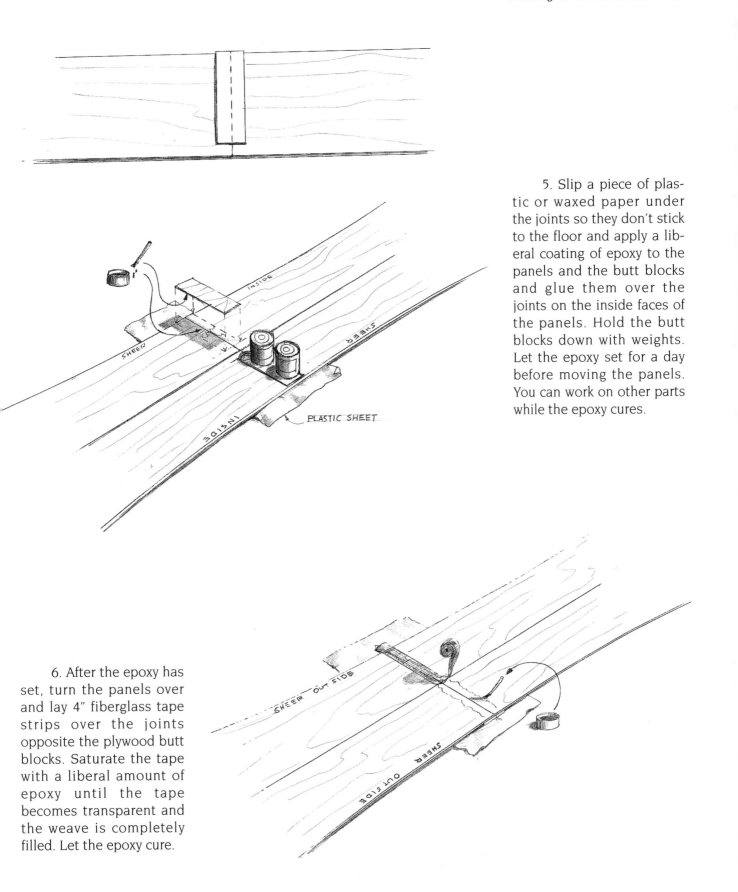

PLASTIC SHEET

5. Slip a piece of plastic or waxed paper under the joints so they don't stick to the floor and apply a liberal coating of epoxy to the panels and the butt blocks and glue them over the joints on the inside faces of the panels. Hold the butt blocks down with weights. Let the epoxy set for a day before moving the panels. You can work on other parts while the epoxy cures.

6. After the epoxy has set, turn the panels over and lay 4" fiberglass tape strips over the joints opposite the plywood butt blocks. Saturate the tape with a liberal amount of epoxy until the tape becomes transparent and the weave is completely filled. Let the epoxy cure.

D. *Constructing the frames*

1. Using the pattern on the plans as a reference, measure out four gussets on scrap pieces of 1/4" plywood. Cut the pieces out and plane and sand them to the lines.

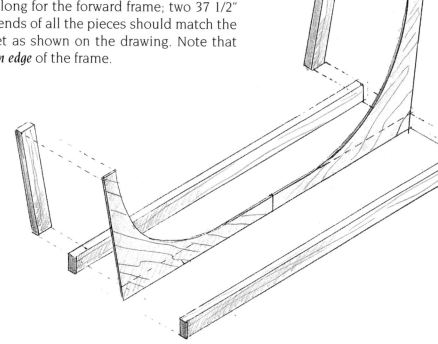

2. Cut four pieces of 1 x 2: two 36" long for the forward frame; two 37 1/2" long for the aft frame. The angles at the ends of all the pieces should match the angle of the straight edges of the gusset as shown on the drawing. Note that the measurements are taken at the *bottom edge* of the frame.

3. Cut out four pieces of 1 x 2 each 13" with the same angle as the gusset at one end of each 1 x 2 piece. These will be the frame uprights and they will be a little longer than ultimately necessary.

4. Lay out the pieces on plastic and glue two gussets between the two 36" pieces as shown and clamp until the epoxy sets. Do the same with the 37 1/2" pieces and the remaining gussets.

5. After the epoxy sets, apply epoxy and clamp the frame uprights to the gussets as shown. Let the epoxy set.

6. Mark the 36" frame "forward" and the 37 1/2" frame "aft" for future reference. Note: later, when installing the frames you'll need to cut notches for the chine logs, but don't do that yet.

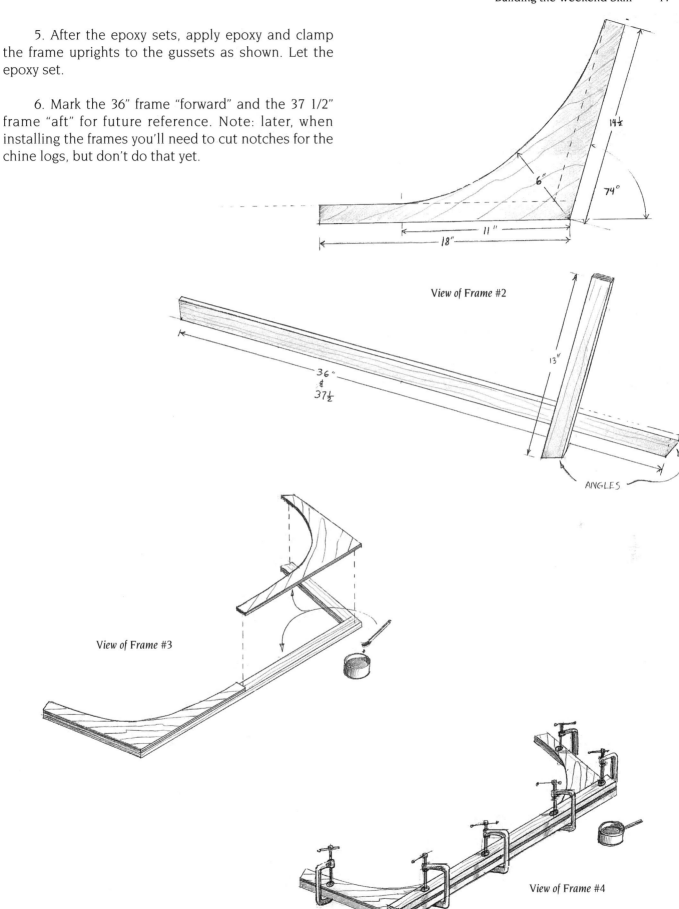

View of Frame #2

View of Frame #3

View of Frame #4

E. *Constructing the transom*

Note: If you are building the outboard skiff be sure to refer to the section on the outboard version and use the measurements for that particular transom as it is wider than the skiff transom and has battens around all edges to carry the thrust of the motor. If you are building the sailing skiff you will cut a notch in the lower transom batten to accept the keelson.

1. Using the drawings as a reference transfer the dimensions to a piece of 1/4" plywood and cut out the transom with a saber saw. We like to develop a nice curve or notch in the top of the transom and John has drawn several possibilities. But you can design your own.

2. Mark and cut 1" x 4" battens, fitting them around the transom bottom and sides of the rowing and sailing skiffs and across the top for the outboard skiff. **Note: *If you are building the sailing skiff, cut a 3/4" high x 3 1/2" wide notch in the center of bottom edge of the lower batten.***

3. Attach with epoxy and ring nails the 3/4" x 3 1/2" battens around the edges and bottom as shown allowing the battens to extend beyond the transom edges about 1/4". Space your ring nails about 2" apart and stagger them as shown. Or, you can clamp or use weight to hold the pieces in place until the epoxy cures.

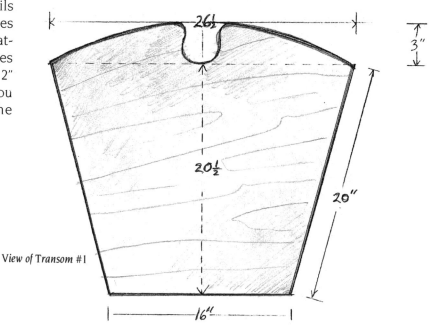

View of Transom #1

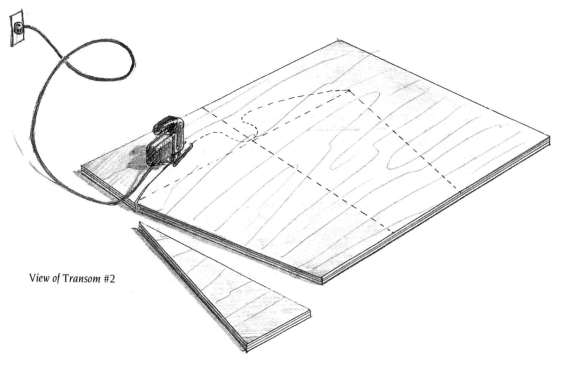

View of Transom #2

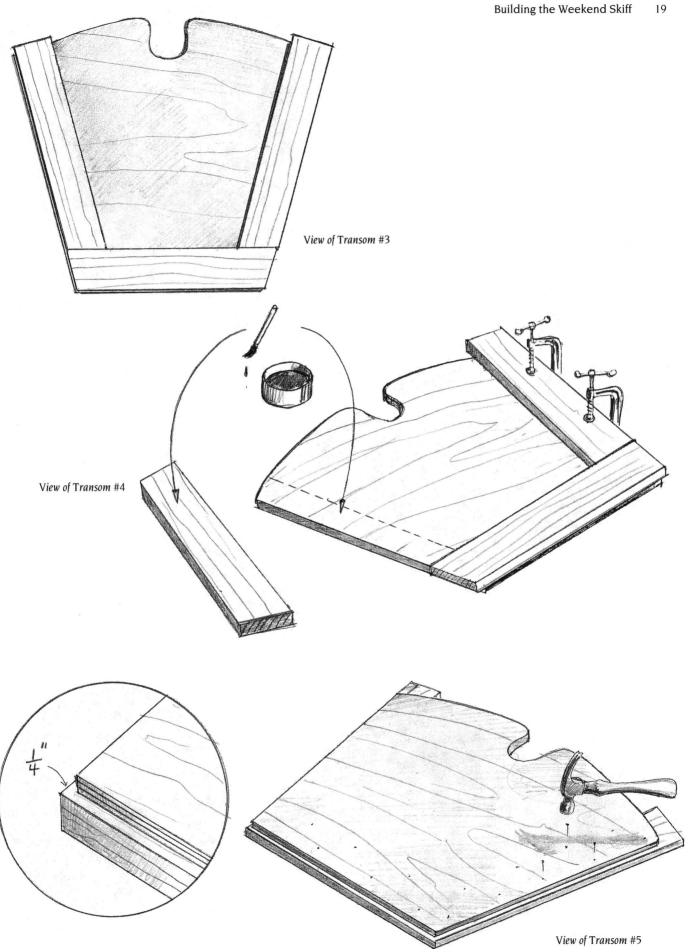

View of Transom #3

View of Transom #4

View of Transom #5

F. Half frames

1. Cut two 13" pieces of 3/4" x 1 1/2" stock for the center half frames. Cut a 3/4" deep by 1 1/2" high notch on one end of each so the half frames can fit over the chine logs.

2. Cut four 12" pieces of 3/4" x 3/4" stock for the fore and aft half frames. These do not have to be notched.

G. Chine logs, gunwales and seat risers
— all taken from 16' lengths

1. Either use store bought 1 x 2's or rip the chine logs to 3/4" x 1 1/2" with a bevel cut to match the angle between the sides and the bottom at the midship point as shown. You can take the angle from the forward frame. If you use i x 2's from the lumber yard you will install them and plane the bevel, in a later step, once they are glued in the boat.

2. Rip the gunwales and seat risers to 3/4" x 1 1/2". There is no bevel on these pieces.

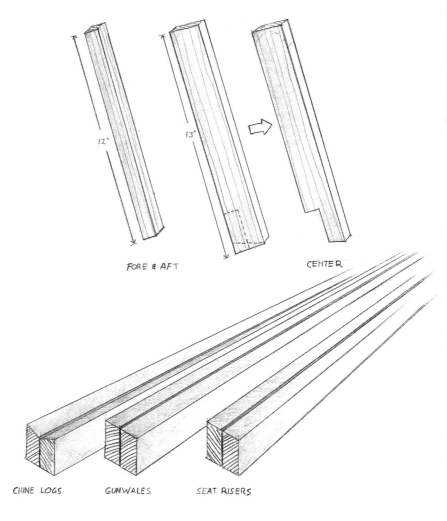

FORE & AFT   CENTER

CHINE LOGS   GUNWALES   SEAT RISERS

Part II: Assembling the Hull

A. Laying down and marking out

Lay out the hull panels on the floor with the bottom edges facing each other and note the positions of the frames and half frames using the drawings as a guide if you haven't already marked them. (Be sure the bows and sterns are matched up or you'll have a funny looking boat.) While the panels are on the floor lay the frames and half frames in position and mark the glue lines with a pencil.

B. Dry assembly

(In this step you assemble the boat without glue so you can be sure alignment is okay and so you can take some angles. Then you will take it apart, one piece at a time to plane angles and, finally to apply epoxy and fasten it permanently.)

1. Attach the stem to one panel with three drywall screws being careful to align the front edges.

2. Drill screw holes for the frames within the glue lines as indicated in the illustrations. Start at the sheer edge and measure 2, 4, 6, 8 and 10 inches and drill a 1/8" hole at each point in the center of the glue area.

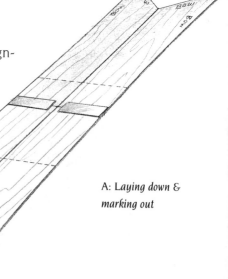

A: Laying down & marking out

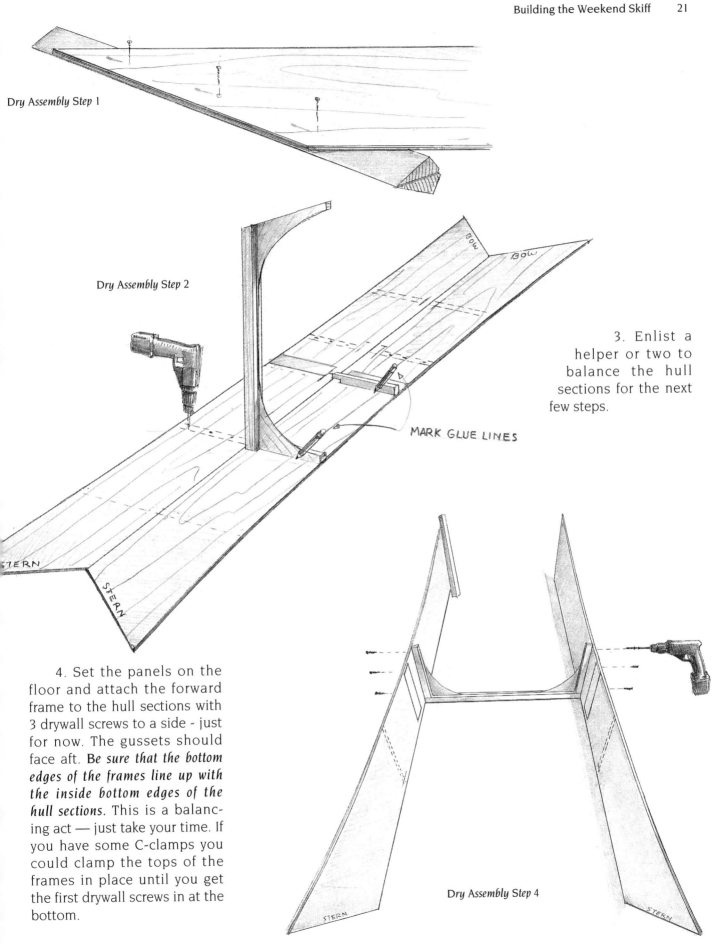

Dry Assembly Step 1

Dry Assembly Step 2

MARK GLUE LINES

3. Enlist a helper or two to balance the hull sections for the next few steps.

4. Set the panels on the floor and attach the forward frame to the hull sections with 3 drywall screws to a side - just for now. The gussets should face aft. *Be sure that the bottom edges of the frames line up with the inside bottom edges of the hull sections.* This is a balancing act — just take your time. If you have some C-clamps you could clamp the tops of the frames in place until you get the first drywall screws in at the bottom.

Dry Assembly Step 4

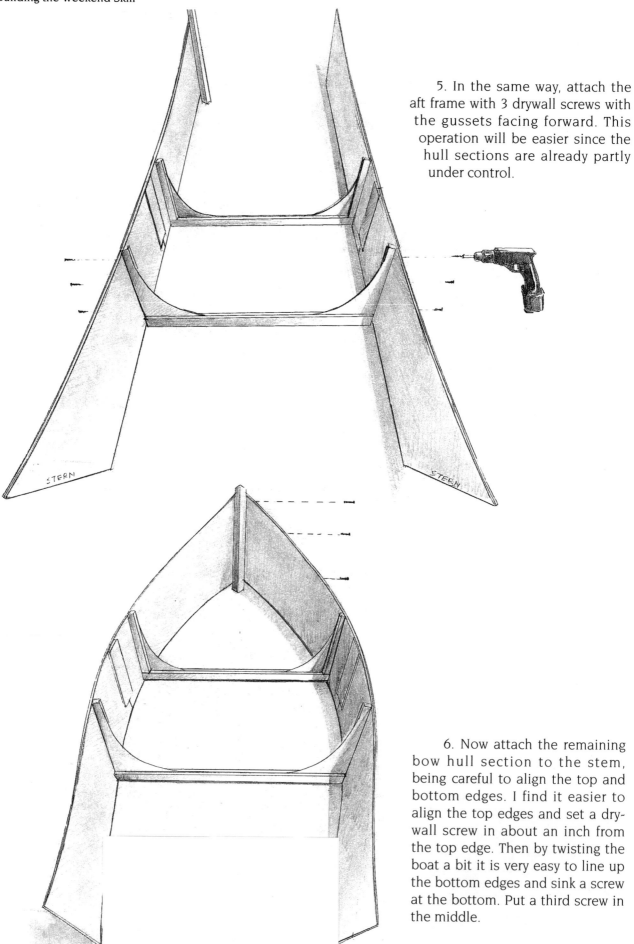

5. In the same way, attach the aft frame with 3 drywall screws with the gussets facing forward. This operation will be easier since the hull sections are already partly under control.

6. Now attach the remaining bow hull section to the stem, being careful to align the top and bottom edges. I find it easier to align the top edges and set a drywall screw in about an inch from the top edge. Then by twisting the boat a bit it is very easy to line up the bottom edges and sink a screw at the bottom. Put a third screw in the middle.

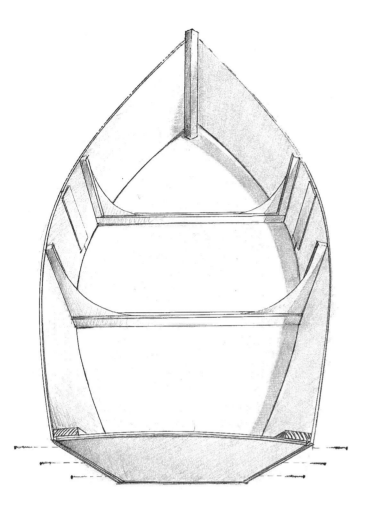

7. Now, you can set the boat up on some wide horses for a more comfortable job. Attach the transom with three drywall screws on each edge.

8. Check the alignment and adjust it if necessary.

Now take a look at your boat — maybe this is a good time to sit down in that builder's chair to appreciate what you've done while you enjoy a cup of coffee

C. *Planing the frames and cutting the notches for the chine logs.*

In this step you'll plane the frame uprights so they fit tightly to the hull sides and then you'll cut notches for the chine logs. **Note: *If you are building the sailing skiff you will need to cut notches in the center of the frames for the keelson.***

1. Cut a scrap piece of stock 38″ long. You'll use it as a spreader in a minute.

2. Using a sliding T-bevel, take the angle of the hull side to a forward frame upright as shown in the illustration. You'll note that there is a gap in the aft edges of the uprights which will defeat any attempt to achieve a tight glue joint.

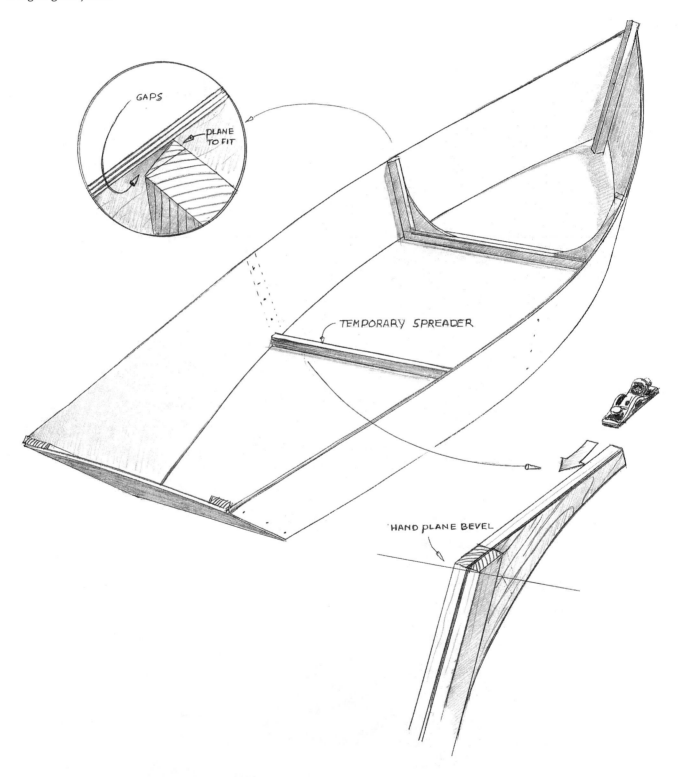

GAPS

PLANE
TO FIT

TEMPORARY SPREADER

HAND PLANE BEVEL

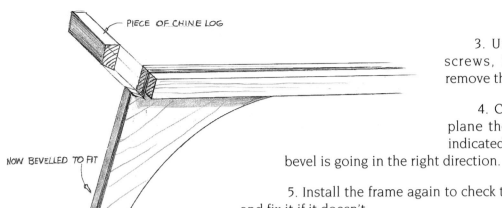

PIECE OF CHINE LOG

NOW BEVELLED TO FIT

3. Unscrew the forward frame screws, insert the spreader and remove the frame.

4. Clamp the frame down and plane the uprights to the angle as indicated by the T-bevel. Be sure the bevel is going in the right direction.

5. Install the frame again to check that it fits properly. Remove and fix it if it doesn't.

6. Remove the frame again and mark out notches for the chine logs using a piece of chine log as shown in the illustration. Cut the notches out.

7. **For the sailing skiff only**: while the frame is out, lay out and cut a notch for the keelson to pass through the lower edge of the frame. The notch measures 3/12" wide and 3/4" deep, (or the width and thickness of your keelson), and is centered on the lower edge of the frame.

8. Repeat steps 2 - 7 for the aft frame.

D. *Fitting the transom.*

In this step you'll plane angles on the sides and bottom of the transom.

1. Using the T-bevel take the angle of the hull side panel to the transom as shown. Remove the transom and plane the angle on each side of the transom. Put the transom back in and check the fit. The hull panels should lay flat on the edges of the transom.

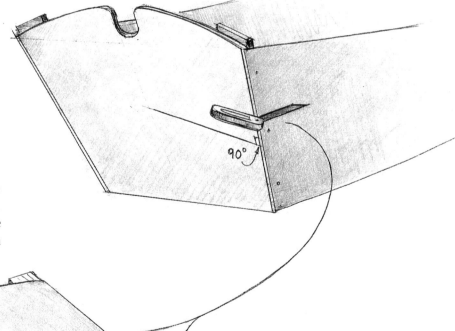

90°

90°

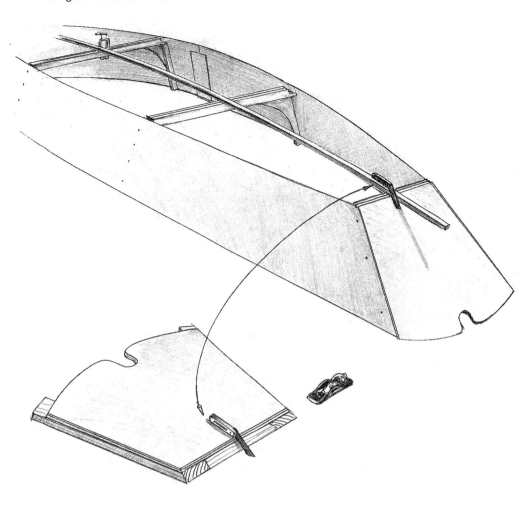

2. Turn the boat upside-down and lay the batten over the bottom so it lays over the aft frame and the bottom of the transom. Use the T-bevel to take the angle of the batten to the transom as shown.

3. Take the transom off and plane the angle.

4. Re-install the transom.

E. *Gluing*

In this step you will use fastenings and epoxy to permanently fasten the pieces you just dry fitted.

1. Remove the drywall screws, one side at a time, glue the stem in place and nail with 10 - 12 ring nails to a side. I find it easier to hold a heavy hammer or piece of wood on the other side to back up the blows. Or, since ring nails are tough to control, you can pre-drill for the ring nails with a 1/16" drill bit. If you decide to pre-drill you should do so before taking the boat apart. In laying out the nail pattern I recommend a zig-zag pattern so you get maximum closure on the stem joint.

Because the ring nails are soft, they bend easily. If one starts to go, stop nailing and pull it out. Don't keep going and hope to fix it later. And, use a finishing hammer to set the nails flush with the surface.

Check for tight fit and add nails if necessary.

2. Remove the forward frame, apply epoxy, and screw it in place with five 3/4" stainless steel screws per side, sinking the heads. Use the spreader to keep the sides apart while the frame is out. Be careful when driving the screws not to drive too hard or you'll strip out the holes and reduce the screws' holding power.

3. Remove the aft frame, apply epoxy and fasten as in # 2.

4. Remove the transom, apply epoxy and nail in place with 8 - 10 ring nails per side.

5. Check fit, tightness of joints and wipe off excess glue.

F. *Chine logs*

In this section you will fit the chine logs — probably the most demanding part of the building process. Read this entire section before starting and refer to John's detailed illustrations.

1. Turn the boat upside down and lay the chine logs over the bottom so you can check that the beveled edges are facing up and that the bevels are angled the right way.

2. At the bow, take the angle of the bottom edge of a hull side panel to the stem with the T-bevel. Cut this angle on the forward ends of the chine logs. Repeat this process at the stern with the transom angle. Don't worry that the chine logs are too long.

3. Insert one chine log at the bow and fit it into the frame notches letting it hang over at the stern. Pull it up flush with the bottom edge of the hull and clamp it with four or five clamps. Check that the angle you cut fits at the bow and re-cut if necessary and reinstall the chine log as already described.

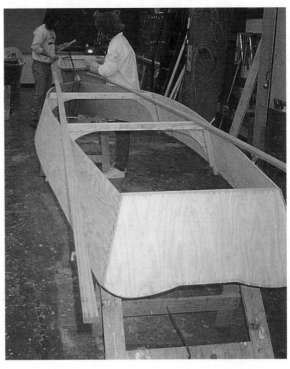

Chine Logs step 1

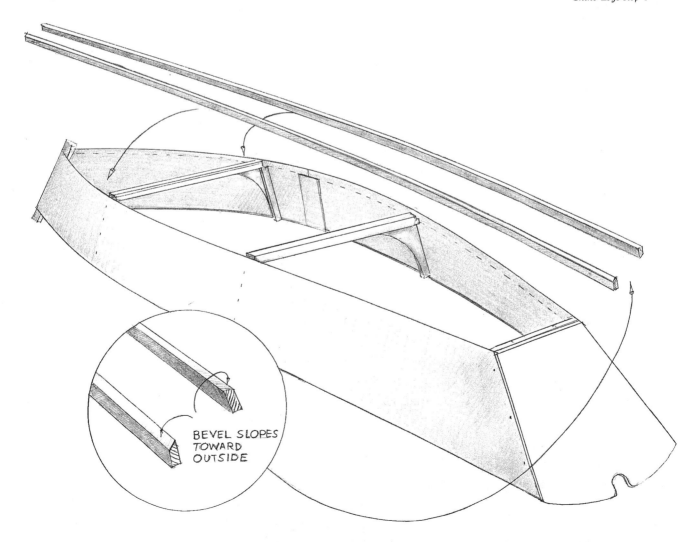

BEVEL SLOPES
TOWARD
OUTSIDE

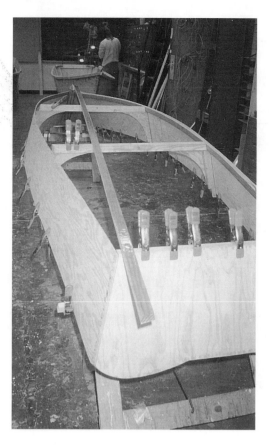

4. Make a pencil line across the chine log at the forward edge of the aft frame.

5. Pull the chine log out and reinstall it with the end fitting tightly at the transom, making sure the angle fits properly. Pull it up flush as before and clamp.

6. Mark a line across the chine log at the forward edge of the aft frame. The distance between the two lines you marked is the length you have to cut off to get the chine log to fit.

7. Cut off the excess stock, refit the chine log and clamp it into place. (If the fit isn't perfect, don't worry. (Note: if you are building the sailing skiff, save the chine log cutoffs.) You can go back and fill the ends with thickened epoxy later if the chine logs are an 1/8" -1/4" too short or, if they are too long, recut them to the proper length. If you really cut them short — say an inch or more — you may want to try again with new pieces since the chine logs provide the water seal on the bottom edge.)

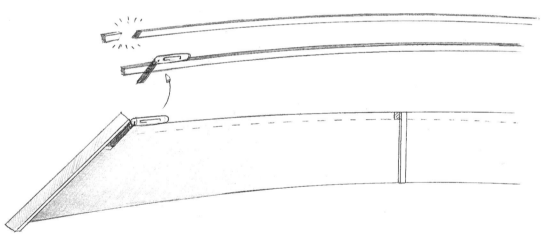

Chine Logs step 2

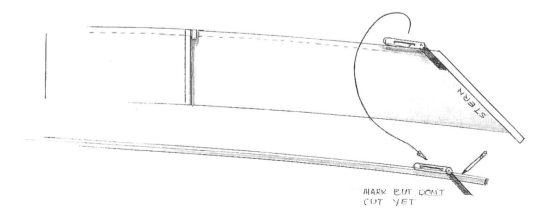

MARK BUT DON'T
CUT YET

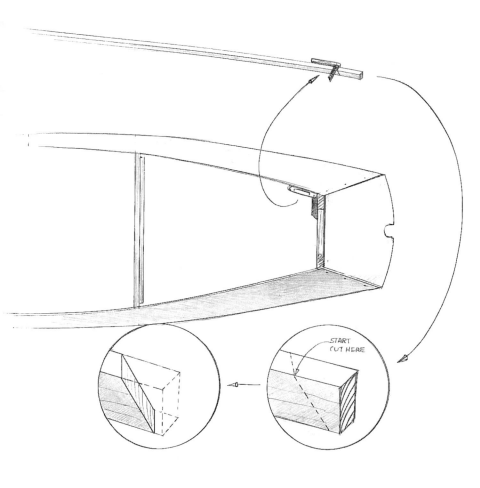

8. Repeat this process with the other side. (*Illustrations continue on page* 30.)

9. Draw glue lines, remove the chine logs, wet out the surfaces with epoxy. Then, apply a second coat of epoxy thickened with wood flour or Cabosil right away and nail or clamp the chine log in place, one side at a time. The thickened epoxy insures a tight bond. Locate nails every 3". Turn the boat over and wipe off excess glue.

Chine Logs step 2 continued

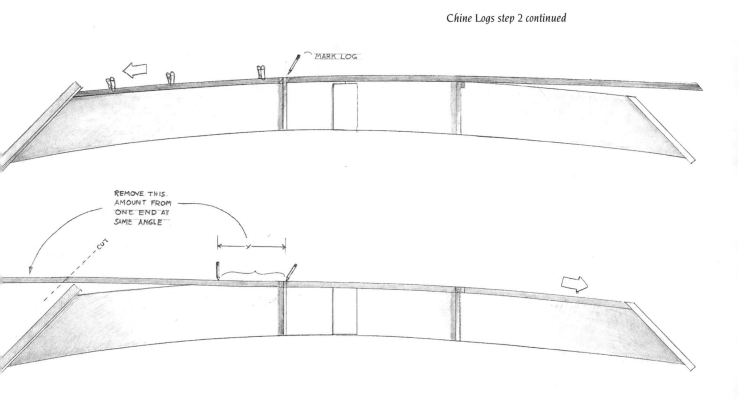

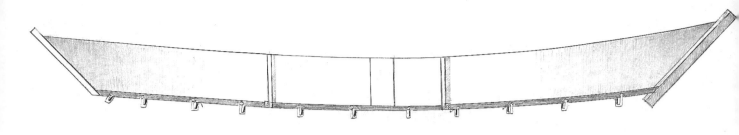

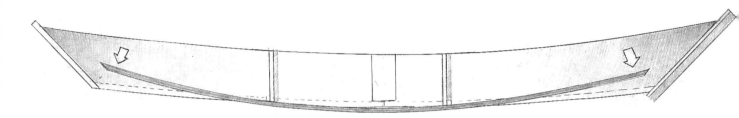

G. Bottom

In this section you will plane the bottom edges of the boat flat to insure that the bottom panels lay flat for a tight gluing surface. Then you will glue and nail the bottom pieces on.

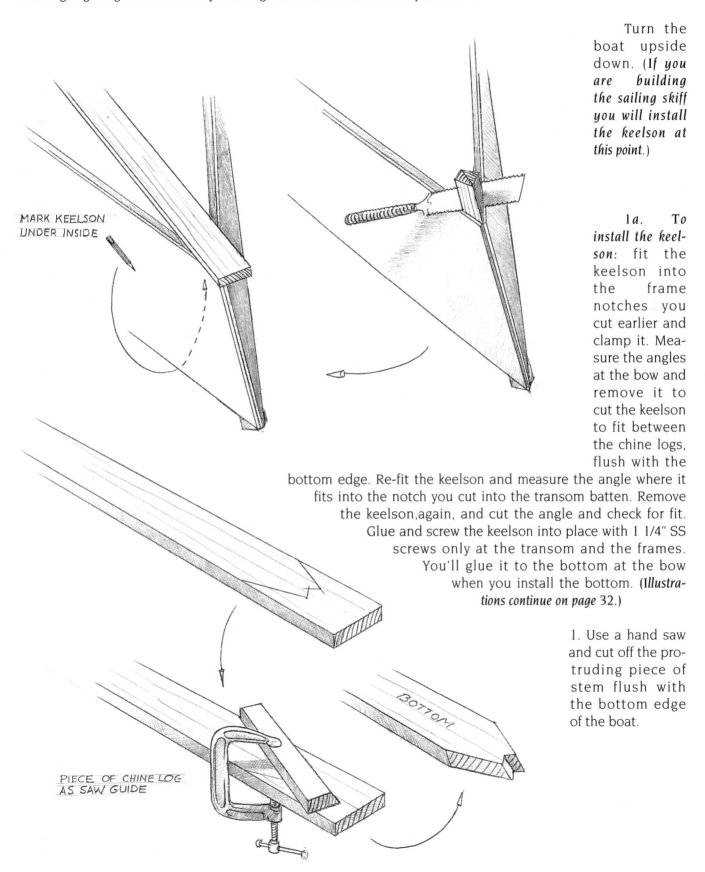

MARK KEELSON UNDER INSIDE

PIECE OF CHINE LOG AS SAW GUIDE

BOTTOM

Turn the boat upside down. (*If you are building the sailing skiff you will install the keelson at this point.*)

1a. *To install the keelson*: fit the keelson into the frame notches you cut earlier and clamp it. Measure the angles at the bow and remove it to cut the keelson to fit between the chine logs, flush with the bottom edge. Re-fit the keelson and measure the angle where it fits into the notch you cut into the transom batten. Remove the keelson, again, and cut the angle and check for fit. Glue and screw the keelson into place with 1 1/4" SS screws only at the transom and the frames. You'll glue it to the bottom at the bow when you install the bottom. (*Illustrations continue on page 32.*)

1. Use a hand saw and cut off the protruding piece of stem flush with the bottom edge of the boat.

2. Using your low angle block plane, plane the chine logs and hull panel edges flush and flat so a straight edge, placed across the boat at the bottom edges, will lay flat at any point. If necessary plane the bottoms of the frames and the transom to insure that the straight-edge lays flat and on the same plane as the chine logs. This step is necessary so your bottom panel will lay flat and seal properly to the chine logs.

3. Use contact cement to glue your # 50 sandpaper to a 40" piece of 2" x 4" and use this sanding board to fine tune your edge planning. Lay the sanding board across the boat and move it back and forth. This tool will true the edges and leave some "tooth" for the epoxy to bite into when you glue up.

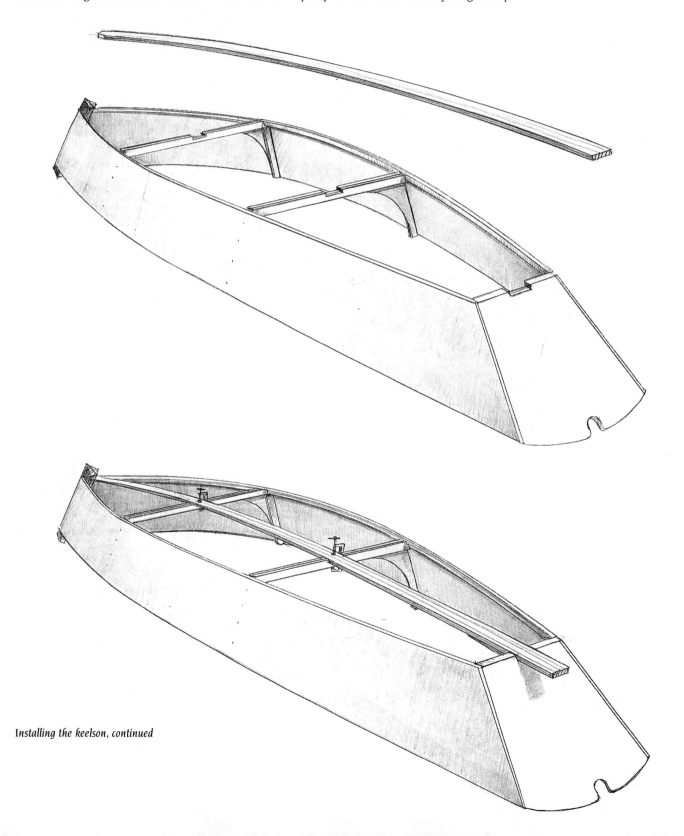

Installing the keelson, continued

Installing the bottom, steps 2 & 3

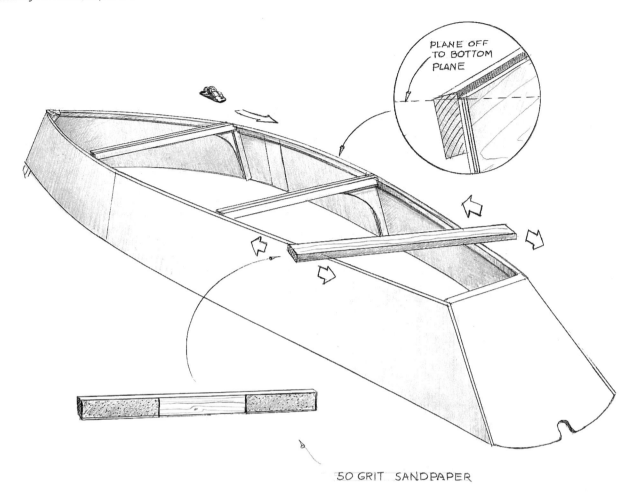

PLANE OFF
TO BOTTOM
PLANE

50 GRIT SANDPAPER

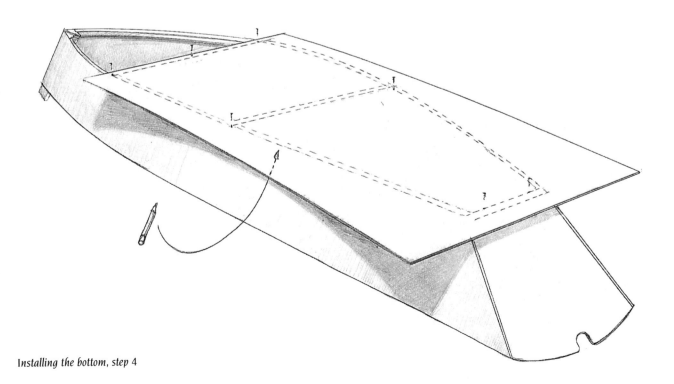

Installing the bottom, step 4

4. Lay a plywood panel on the aft part of the boat aligning the forward edge at the middle of the forward frame. Attach temporarily with 6 drywall screws driven into the chine logs. Scribe a glue line on the inside and cutting line on the outside of the bottom panel.

5. Remove the panel and cut out the bottom shape with a saber saw leaving about a 1/8" - 1/4" overlap.

6. Apply epoxy to both the chine log edges, keelson (if you have one) the frame bottoms and the bottom. Add thickened epoxy to one gluing surface.

7. Reattach the bottom with the drywall screws to hold it in place and nail the bottom with ring nails set in from the edge about 3/4" and spaced 2" apart.
Be sure to nail across the aft and forward frames and the keelson. Refer to the illustrations to see how to use a marking gauge for the nailing line.

8. Turn the boat over, check joints and wipe off the excess glue.

9. Butt the second panel against the first and repeat the process as in steps 4 -8.

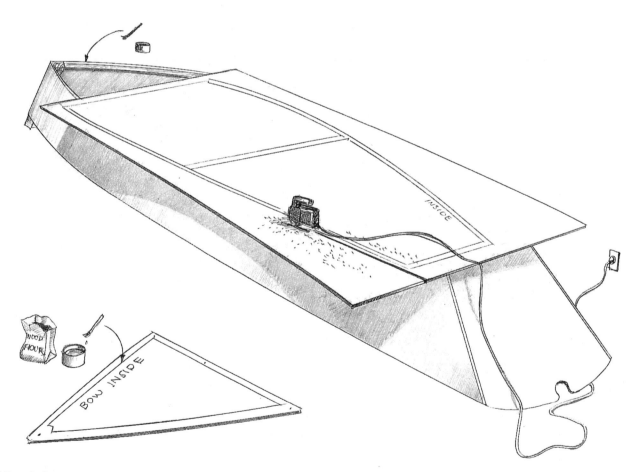

Installing the bottom, step 5

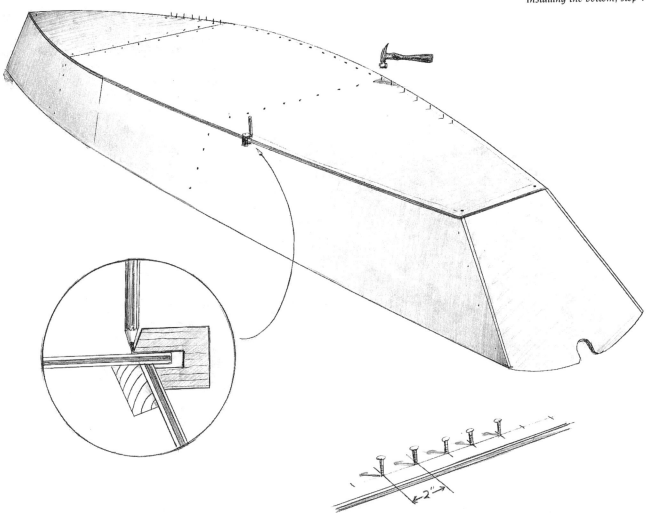

H. *Gunwales*

1. With the boat upright, clamp a gunwale along the sheer line, scribe a glue line and remove. Bend the gunwales carefully so the stress doesn't crack them. This is particularly necessary if you have knots in the wood.

2. Apply epoxy to both faces, re-clamp and nail or screw the gunwale in place locating the nails or screws every 6".

3. Countersink 1 1/4" # 8 stainless steel screws at the ends into the stem and transom.

4. Wipe off excess glue and cut off excess stock to match the angles at the stem and transom.

5. Repeat steps 1 - 4 for the other side.

I. Half-Frames

The half-frames help support the longitudinal risers that, in turn, support the seats. When you laid out the panels you marked the positions of the half-frames. If you missed that step go back to the plans and locate their positions. Remember: the half-frames are perpendicular to the bottom edge.

1. The center half-frames are cut from the 1" x 2" stock and are notched over the chine logs. Install one on each side with epoxy and four 3/4" stainless steel screws attached from the outside.

2. The fore and aft half-frames are cut from 3/4" x3/4" stock. Locate them and glue and screw them in place.

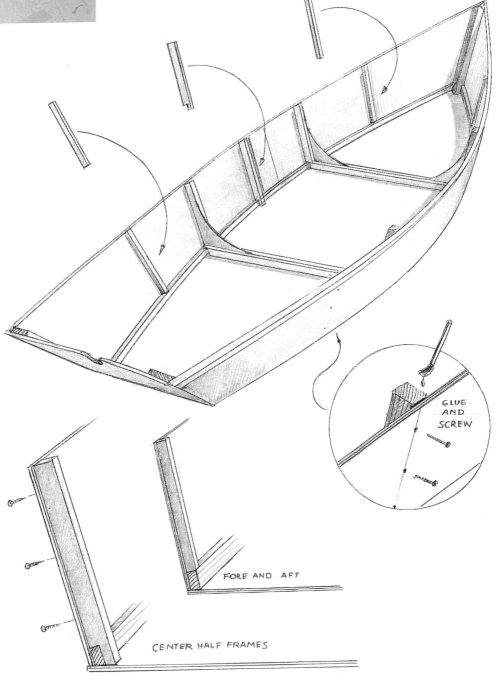

GLUE AND SCREW

FORE AND AFT

CENTER HALF FRAMES

J. Keel

Note: Omit this step if you are building the sailing skiff.

1. Mark a center line along the length of the boat and drill 1/8" holes every 6" along this line.

2. Attach a 1" x 1" keel piece with epoxy and 3/4" stainless steel screws.

3. Trim off the keel at the bow and stern and plane a taper at the bow. You may want to remove a few screws at the bow after the epoxy cures to avoid damaging the plane.

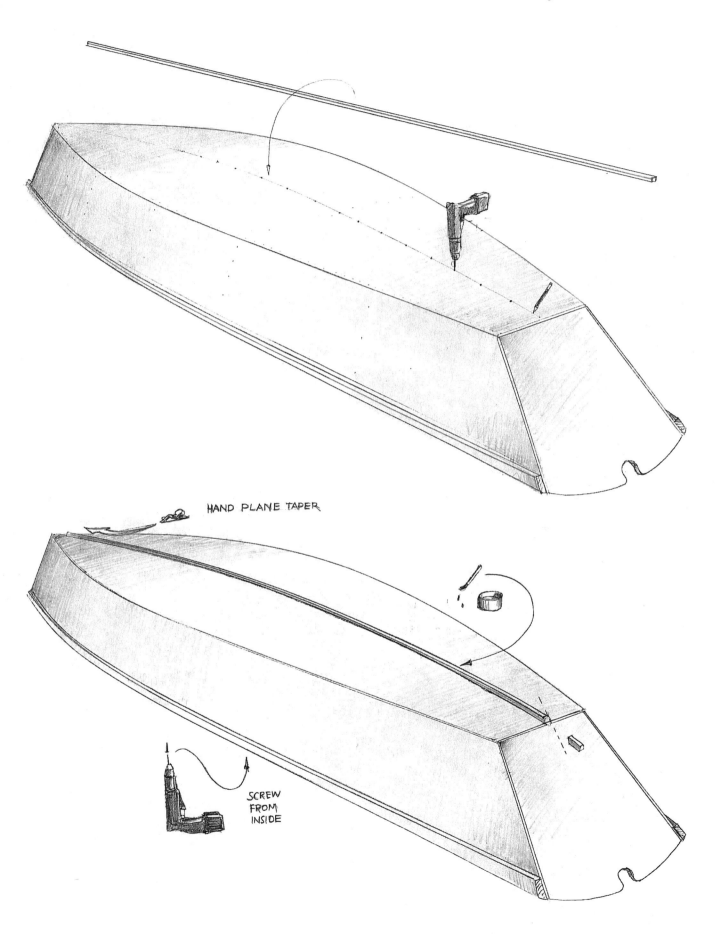

HAND PLANE TAPER

SCREW FROM INSIDE

K. *Seat risers*

The seat risers are longitudinal seat support members that are screwed to the frames, half-frames and to the hull at each end). The risers are cut from 1" x 2" stock.

1. Cut a spacing block out of scrap 9" long. Use this spacer to locate where to mark a line on each frame and half-frame 9" up from the bottom (not the chine log) of the boat. This mark locates the top of the riser.

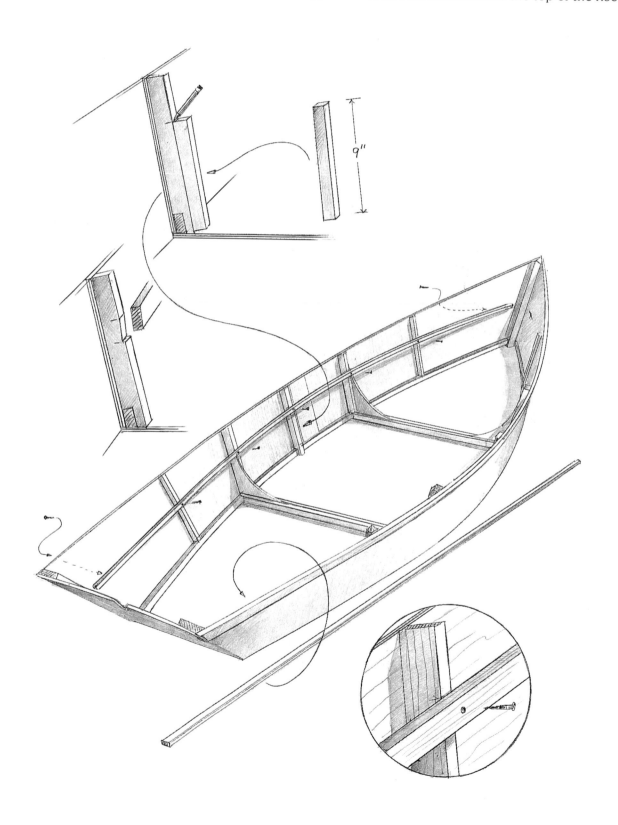

2. Make similar marks at the ends of the boat on the sides of the hull about 2" from the stem and transom. This marks the height of the risers at each end of the boat.

3. On the full frames you may have to cut notches in the gussets so the risers can lay flat against the frame. You can use a cut-off piece of 1" x 2" stock as a guide in marking for the notches. Remember, though, that the risers fit below the 9" marks.

4. Measure the boat for the risers by stretching a tape measure along the inside of the sides at the the 9" height you've already marked. Start the measurement 2" from the stem and end it 2" from the transom. This should give a measurement that is *about* 13' 6". Cut the risers from 1"x 2" stock to the correct length.

5. Dry fit the risers into place, screwing them into the frames and half-frames with 1 1/4" # 8 stainless steel screws. Before screwing in the ends you may want to lay a piece of scrap across the two risers at the bow and the stern, simulating seats, to check that the seat won't rock on uneven risers and adjust as necessary. Then secure the ends of the risers directly to the hull by driving 3/4" SS screws in from the outside.

L. Seats

There are a number of seating suggestions illustrated. You can use our suggestions or devise your own. *Note: If you are building the sailing skiff you need to refer to that section for seat layout because the seats act as braces for the mast and centerboard trunk.*

1. Referring to the drawings, locate, measure and cut the center seat out of 1" x 10" stock. Glue and screw a 1" x 1" strengthening batten down the center of the underside of the seat leaving about 1 1/2" spaces at the ends so the seat batten will fit between the risers.

2. Fasten the seat in place with three 1 1/4" # 8 SS screws at each end, driven into the risers. Don't glue the risers or the seats in place.

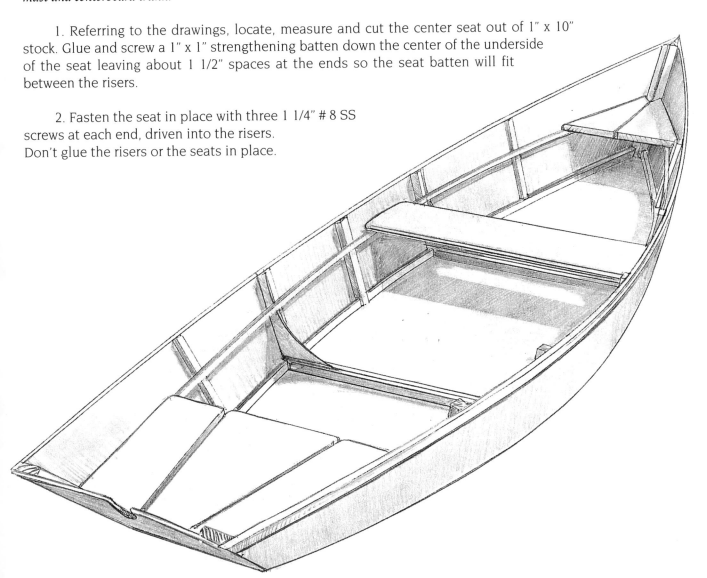

3. As indicated on the drawings, or following your own design, cut the pieces for the stern seat and fasten it to the risers with stainless steel screws.

4. Repeat this process for the bow seat.

5. Remove the seats and risers, sand with # 80 and # 120 sandpaper and apply several coats of varnish and set aside. (With the risers and seats out it will be easier to paint the inside of the boat. *See Part IV Finishing and Part V: Installing the Seats.*)

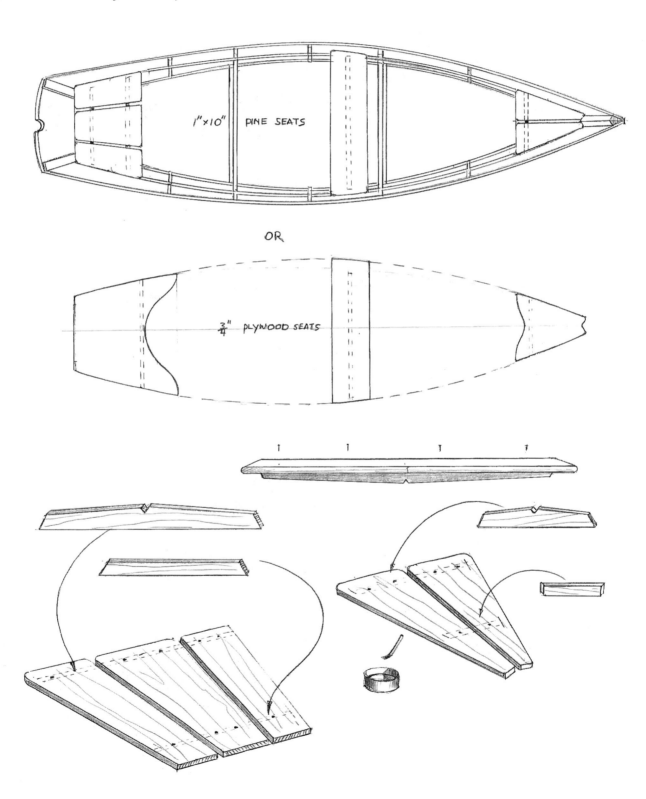

M. *Floorboards* (Optional)

To save wear and tear on the bottom you can install cedar floorboards between the frames and at each end. Use 1/2" x 3" stock and run the floorboards fore and aft over 1" x 3/4" cross-battens. Do not fasten these in place so they can be removed easily for bailing and cleaning.

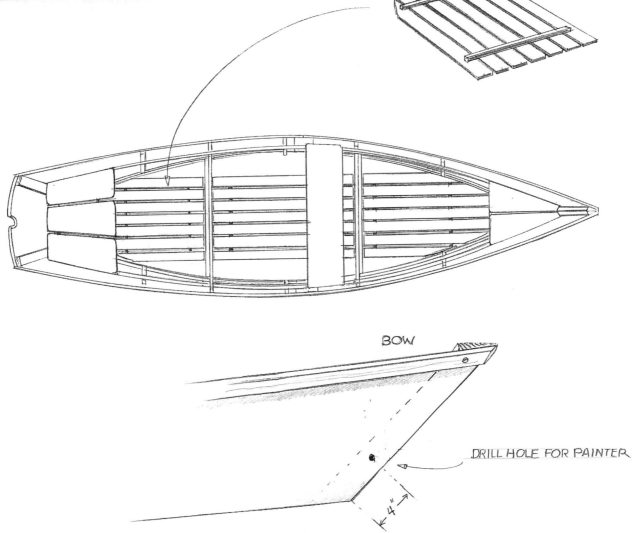

BOW

DRILL HOLE FOR PAINTER

4"

Part III: Filling and Sanding

A. *Filling*

Remove any drywall screws left in the boat as these were just temporary fastenings.

Mix up some epoxy and add wood flour to the consistency of peanut butter. Using a plastic putty knife or scraper, (an old credit card works great) , fill in all holes and dings, being careful not to leave too much excess that will have to be sanded off later. If the epoxy mixture "sags"out of a hole you can put a duct tape "band aid" on it to keep it in place. The duct tape doesn't stick to the epoxy and can be peeled off easily.

If you see any gaps along the chine logs where they meet the bottom you can use the thickened epoxy mixture to make fillet. Tip the boat to one side to keep the epoxy fillet in place if necessary or use the duct tape to contain it. Again, don't get carried away with this stuff as it is a bear to sand out when it hardens.

B. *Trimming and rounding off*

1. Cut off excess stock from the tops of the frames and half-frames and round off the ends. To make a consistent job of it you may want to make a rounding pattern from a piece of scrap and trace the pattern on all the pieces that need rounding off.

2. Cut off the stem end and sand it smooth, blending it into the gunwale. Then sand off the gunwale ends with coarse sandpaper on a block.

3. Use your low angle block plane to plane the gunwales, bringing the plywood and gunwales to a consistent surface and rounding off the edges. Use coarse sandpaper to clean up the transom at the top and around the sides and bottom.

4. Turn the boat over and use the plane to trim the bottom edge and finish it off with # 50 , then # 80 sandpaper over a block. For these bottom edges and the stem edge I like to use the # 50 sandpaper glued to a 12" long sanding board made from a scrap piece of 2" x 4". The sanding board really lets you get some muscle into the job and speeds things up - particularly on those troublesome edges. Just be sure the epoxy is completely set so you don't load up the sandpaper with semi-cured epoxy.

5. Now is a good time to locate a hole for the painter (rope to tie up the boat). To avoid splitting the wood, first drill an 1/8" hole through the stem of the boat, from side to side, about 4" from the bottom. Then enlarge this hole to 3/8". Roll up a piece of sandpaper and clean up the hole. Saturate the inside of the hole with epoxy to prevent water absorption.

C. *Sanding*

Now is the time to thoroughly sand the entire boat. Wear a dust mask during this phase as the fine dust can be very irritating.

You can use a power sander or do it by hand, working from # 80 sandpaper to # 120. If you have a random orbit sander this is the ideal tool to use. However, be careful not to over sand keeping in mind that power sanders have a tendency to ripple the surface on fir plywood because of the pronounced hard/soft grain pattern. And, of course, you want to sand with the grain so you can avoid scratches.

In many respects a piece of sandpaper wrapped around a block does the job very well. This can be a great opportunity to involves the kids in the project.

Part IV: Finishing

A. *Option* 1

This is the option for the longest lasting and most professional job. In this option you will coat the entire boat with epoxy and sheath the outside with fiberglass cloth. If you haven't worked with fiberglass before I would recommend that you try a test piece or two to get used to the process. Maybe you could fiberglass a small cardboard box, for example.

1. Mask off the gunwales with good quality masking tape.

2. Turn the boat upside down and cover the hull with 6 ounce fiberglass cloth. Cut darts in the cloth so it lays flat over the transom and sides down to the gunwales. It may hang over a bit at this point. Overlap the cloth about an inch at the stem. Trim it carefully so it fits well.

If possible, enlist a helper for this job so one of you can work on each side of the boat.

3. Mix up about a cup of epoxy and apply it with a foam roller starting at the center line of the boat and working to the edges and over the sides. Saturate the cloth with epoxy and spread it with foam brushes or plastic spreaders until the cloth becomes transparent. Mix more epoxy as needed. To keep it from kicking off too soon it is best to pour it into shallow containers to dissipate the heat that builds when you mix it. This is particularly important in weather over seventy degrees. Don't begin this process if the temperature is less than sixty or over eighty.

Be sure to smooth out the cloth and work out any bubbles as you go. Press the cloth into the corners where the sides meet the gunwales and be sure the stem overlaps lay flat.

With two people, applying each coat should take about 30 minutes.

4. When the epoxy begins to become tacky, apply a fresh coating, spreading it evenly. With this coat the weave will begin to fill up.

5. When the second coat becomes tacky, apply a third coat which should completely fill the weave, leaving a uniform and smooth surface.

6. When this coat becomes tacky, use a utility knife to trim off the excess fiberglass at the gunwales and transom being careful not to lift the cloth. Peel the masking tape off the gunwales carefully.

7. When the epoxy has cured and is no longer sticky, wash the boat down with a 5% ammonia and water solution. When the hull is dry lightly sand the entire boat with # 120 sand- paper. Then wet sand the boat with # 200 wet sandpaper. To wet sand you'll need a bucket of water and a rubber sanding block around which you wrap the sandpaper. Sand the entire surface, dipping the sandpaper in the bucket frequently so the surface is always wet. When you're finished wash down the boat with clear water.

8. Turn the boat over and saturate the inside with epoxy. Wash it down with the ammonia solution and lightly sand it when it is cured. (You don't need to use fiberglass cloth on the inside.)

9. Wipe the boat down with solvent for the paint you are using and, when that dries, paint the boat with marine epoxy paint. Use a foam roller and "tip the paint out", leveling with a wide foam brush. Most epoxy paints do not need a primer if applied over properly prepared fiberglass. But read the label to make sure.

10. When the paint is dry, varnish the gunwales to protect the epoxy.

B. *Option* 2

This is the option for a good serviceable job that balances cost and effort with results. You will saturate the entire boat with epoxy, sand it and paint. But, you will *not* use fiberglass cloth.

1. Mix epoxy in amounts of about a cup or so and pour it into a shallow container. Apply it to the entire surface of the boat, first on the outside, then, after it is cured, on the inside. Use wide foam brushes to apply the epoxy.

2. When the epoxy is no longer tacky, wipe it down with the 5% solution of ammonia and water. Lightly sand the surface with # 120 sandpaper.

3. Apply a second coat of epoxy.

4. When the second coat of epoxy is cured, wash it down with an ammonia and water solution and then wet sand with # 220 sandpaper.

5. Varnish the gunwales over the epoxy with a marine varnish.

6. When the varnish is dry, mask off the gunwales and apply marine paint, following the directions carefully. Remove the masking tape from the gunwales when the paint is still tacky.

C. *Option 3*

This is the option for an inexpensive job that will still be serviceable. It is particularly applicable for school and community programs in which kids are building the boats because it minimizes the use of toxic materials and is easy to clean up.

1. Varnish the gunwales.

2. When the varnish is dry, mask out the gunwales and apply exterior house primer to the entire boat. Use paint rollers for the flat panels and cheap bristle brushes for the corners and edges. Let this primer dry for at least several days before moving to the next step.

3. Paint the boat with latex, satin finish house paint. If possible, let the this coat harden off for at least a week before launching the boat.

Part V: Installing Seats

When you have painted the boat and the paint is dry, you can re-install the seat risers and screw in the seats with 1 1/4" stainless steel screws.

Part VI: Oarlocks, Oars, Motors and flotation.

A. Buy a set of oarlocks that attach to the outside of the gunwales and install them about 12" - 15" aft of the back edge of the middle seat.

B. We've found that a set of 7' oars propels the boat very nicely. You can purchase such oars at prices ranging from $ 30.00 a set to $ 200.00. But, the fact is, that the cheapest ones will work just fine.

C. The outboard motor version is designed for a very small motor of less than 5 hp or for an electric trolling motor. In the section dealing with the outboard motor skiff we'll discuss flotation which should be a part of any boat that requires heavy attachments such as motors and batteries.

SECTION III — OPTIONS:
OUTBOARD MOTOR AND SAILING VERSIONS

In this section you will find suggestions for two variations on the basic rowing skiff.

The outboard skiff is simply the rowing skiff with a wider transom to carry the weight of a small motor and pilot. It also has some additional bracing to counter the twisting forces that even a small motor produces. But, the outboard skiff is still very simple to build and shouldn't produce any problems for the novice builder.

The sailing skiff is a bit more complicated to build because it has a dagger board that requires a tight fitting dagger board case. There is also a keelson on which the dagger board case is mounted.

The sail plan is very simple and conservative to provide an introduction to the joys of sailing. Later, if you want, you can read up on the many alternate rigs and change it to your liking. Right now it employs an unstayed mast that you can step in a minute and a loose-footed lug sail so you don't need a boom. The entire rig stows out of the way in the boat when you don't need it.

A. Suggestions for an outboard powered skiff

Differences from the rowing skiff — the outboard skiff has a wider transom and some additional bracing.

Additional materials needed

2 pcs. 1" x 2" x 16' for optional inwales
1 pc. 6" x 12" x 8' foam flotation material
12 2" x # 8 stainless steel screws for knees and breasthook
scrap pieces of 1" x 10" for quarter
    knees

1. Transom

Refer to the illustration for the wider transom dimensions. Its installation is the same as the transom in the rowing skiff, however, there is a batten around the top edge to accept the motor clamps. (**Illustration for battens on page** 50.)

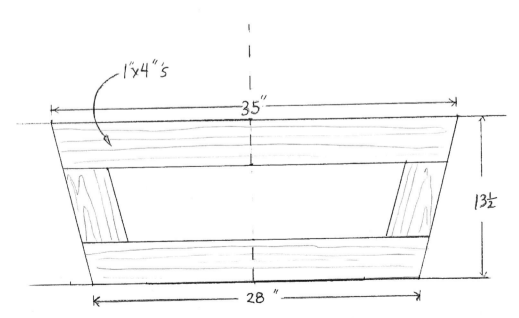

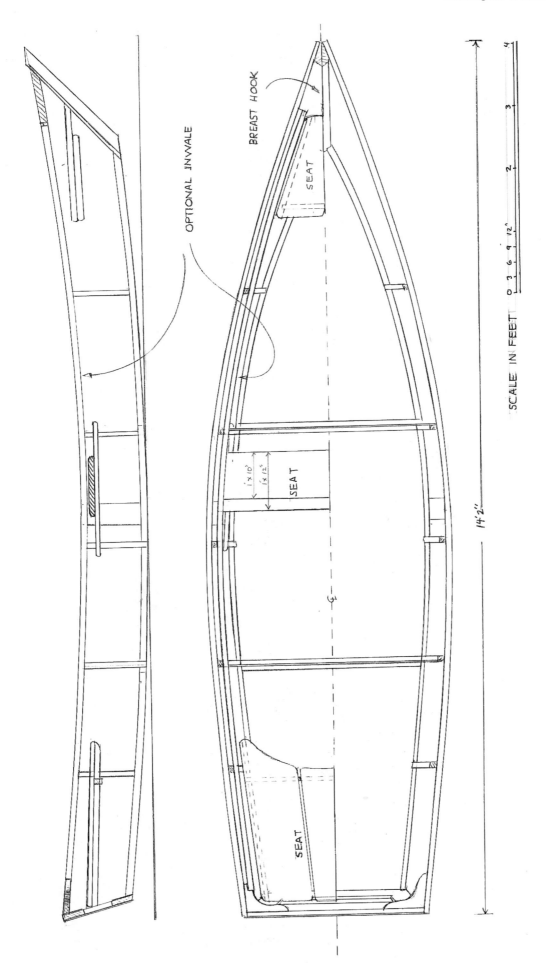

OPTIONAL INWALE

BREAST HOOK

SEAT

1" x 10"
1" x 12"

SEAT

SEAT

3'

14' 2"

SCALE IN FEET

0 3 6 9 12'   1   2   3   4

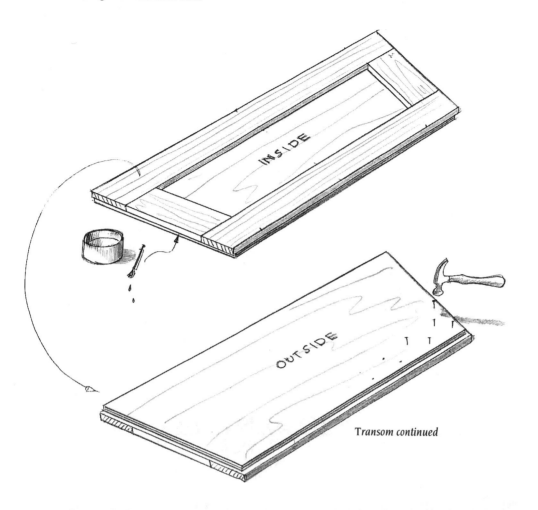

Transom continued

2. Quarter knees

The transom is braced by quarter knees to resist the thrust and twist of the motor. The quarter knees are triangular blocks, measuring about 6" along the edges at the corner where the sides and transom meet. They need to be carefully beveled to fit. If you have access to a belt sander or stationary disc sander it would make this job go faster. Otherwise, clamp the pieces down and use your block plane to rough it out and the coarse sanding board to fine tune the fit.

Install the quarter knees after installing the gunwales using four 2" # 8 stainless steel screws driven from the outside into holes pre-drilled to prevent splitting the wood. Two screws go into each knee from the side, through the gunwale and two go into each knee from the rear through the transom. (*See illustrations on page 51.*)

Quarter knees

3. Breasthook (optional)

This is a triangular piece that fits in the bow at the sheer, just behind the stem. It provides additional stiffness to counter the forces produced by a motor. You can make it out of a piece of 1" x 10" (your seat stock). Fit it carefully — maybe make a pattern out of scrap — and epoxy and screw it in with 4 2" stainless steel screws, predrilled. The breasthook is not necessary if you are only using a small electric trolling motor.

4. Inwales (optional)

Inwales are cut from 1" x 2" stock and are mounted opposite the gunwales, along the inside of the sheer, to provide additional stiffness. These can be notched and screwed to the insides of the frames and notched into the breasthook and quarter knees. Again, I would not bother with them if I were only using a small electric trolling motor on the boat. But, if I were using a gasoline powered outboard I'd install them to help carry the additional weight and thrust.

5. Flotation

Under each seat you should build a 1/4" plywood box which contains foam flotation. This box can be built around pieces of high density foam and fastened to the undersides of the seats. The depth of the boxes should be about 6" to allow access to the floor under the seats. Drill holes in the bottom piece of plywood for each box to allow water to drain out or build the bottom of the boxes with slats.

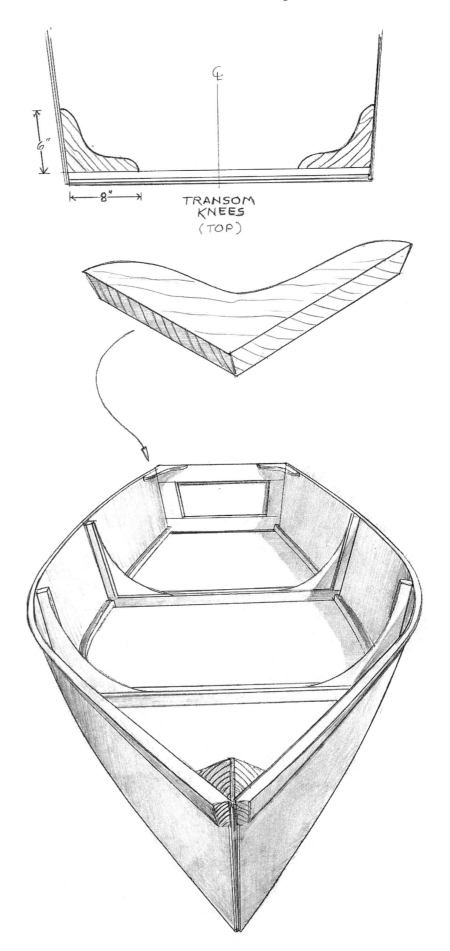

TRANSOM
KNEES
(TOP)

B. Suggestions for a sailing skiff

Differences from the rowing skiff — The sailing skiff has a keelson, a dagger board trunk and dagger board, a skeg, and a rudder. And, the seating plan is different: the forward seat is moved back to so it can function as a mast brace; the middle seat functions as both a seat and thwart or brace for the dagger board trunk. And, of course, you have a mast, a lug and a sail.

Additional materials needed
2 pcs. 2" x 4" x 10' clear pine or spruce for the mast
2 pcs. 1" x 2" x 5' clear pine or spruce for the gaff
1 pcs. 1/2" x 4' x 8' plywood for the dagger board and dagger board case
6 # 10 x 2" stainless steel screws for the skeg
12 # 8 x 2" stainless steel screws for the quarter knees and breasthook
1 3/8" stainless steel bolt 2" long, washers and a jam nut to attach the tiller
4 stainless steel 1/4" eye bolts, washers and nuts to mount the rudder
1 24" piece of 1/4" brass brazing rod to run through the eye bolts or a 3/8" dowel
1 tube of marine adhesive/sealant such as 3M 5200
1 main sail
assorted cleats, shackles and lines

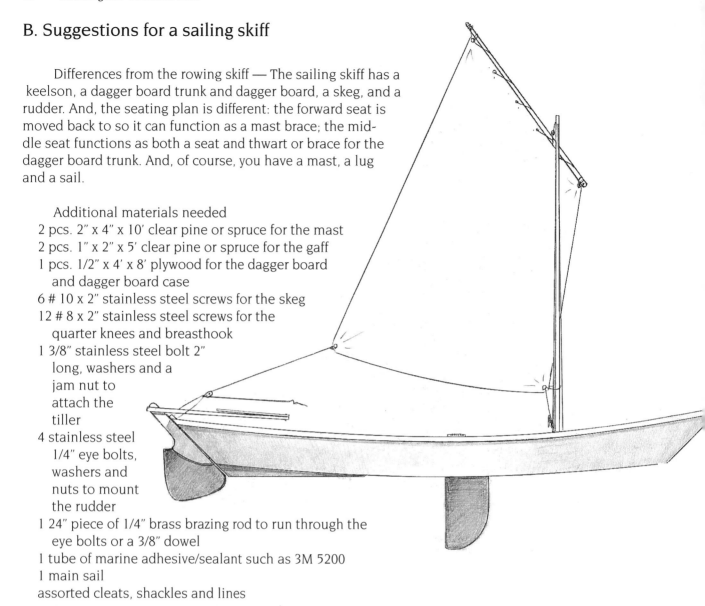

1. Keelson

When constructing the sailing skiff you will install a keelson before putting the bottom on. This has been explained in the main section of the book. The keelson helps support the centerboard and strengthens the bottom.

2. Quarter knees and breasthook (Optional)

Refer to the previous section (A 2 and 3) for instructions on installing quarter knees and a breasthook.

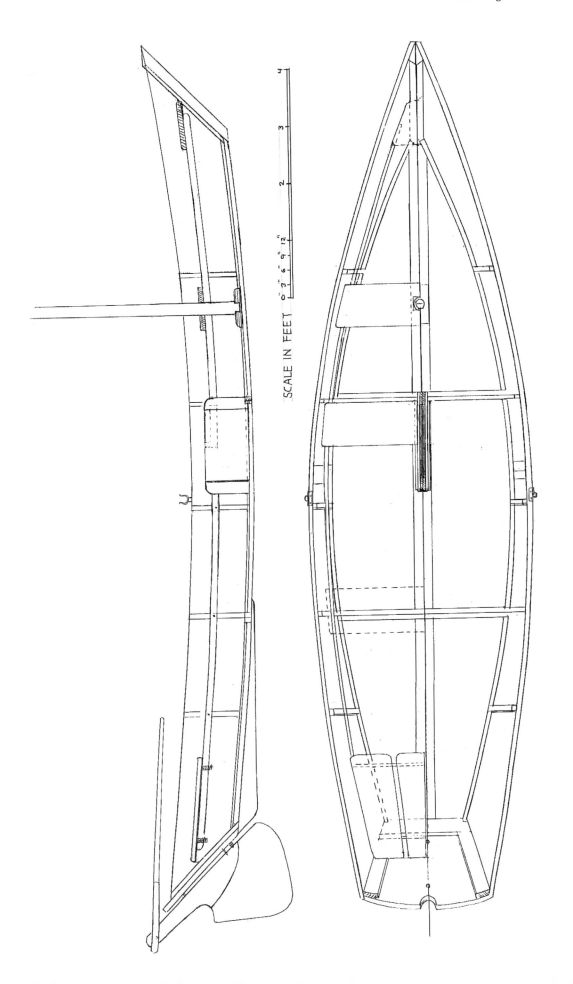

SCALE IN FEET

4

3

2

0" 3" 6" 9" 12"

3. Dagger board trunk

The illustration shows the location and construction of the dagger board trunk which is mounted over a slot cut through the keelson and bottom, just behind the forward frame. Note that there are cleats on each side of the case with the tops positioned 9" from the floor. These cleats support the center seat which will be in two pieces. Install these cleats before you assemble the dagger board case so you can drive the 3/4" screws from what will be the inside of the case. There are also "logs" at the base of the case that enable you to securely mount it on the keelson. These also need to be attached before assembling the case for the same reason.

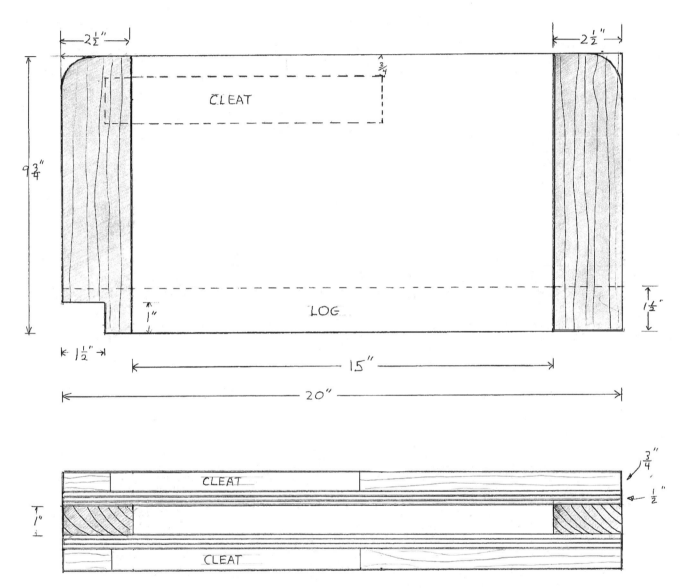

After constructing the dagger board case and attachments, position it on the keelson so you can mark off the curve of the bottom on the bottom edge of the trunk. Plane the bottom of the trunk to fit snugly — this is the major source of leaks in sailboats. You can use coarse sandpaper on a block for the final fitting.

Then mark the location of the slot and cut it out a bit smaller than indicated. Squeeze out an ample bead of marine adhesive/sealant around the slot on the keelson where the trunk will lay. Set the trunk over the slot and screw it into place as indicated in the illustration using 2" stainless steel screws driven in from the bottom. After wiping off the excess sealant, turn the boat over and trim the hole to the exact size of the trunk opening. You can use a wood rasp for this job or you can use a flush-trim bit and a router to speed the job up. **(Illustrations continue on pages 55 and 56.)**

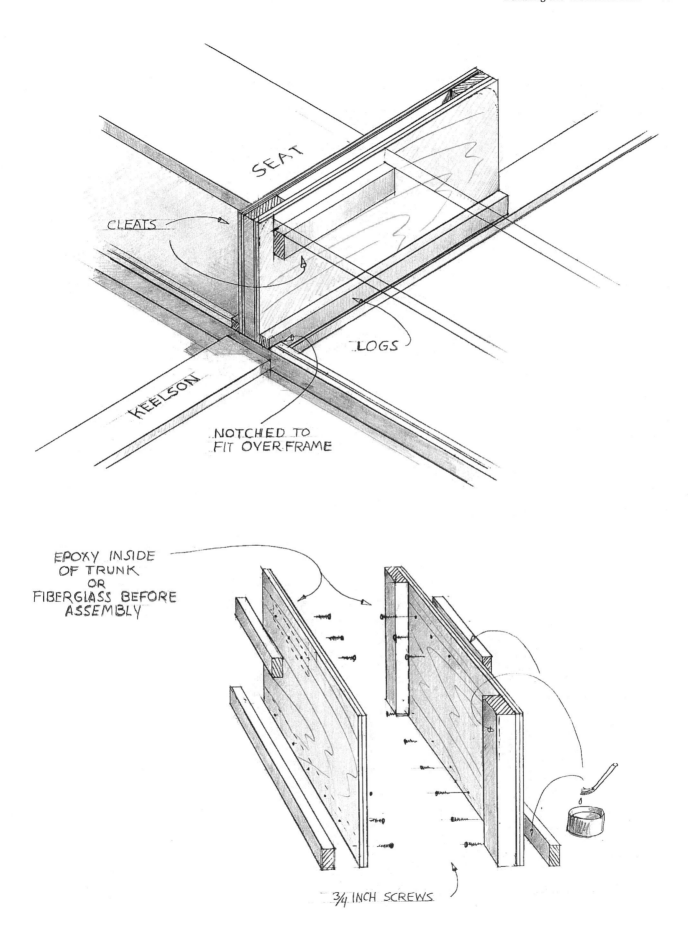

SEAT

CLEATS

LOGS

KEELSON

NOTCHED TO
FIT OVER FRAME

EPOXY INSIDE
OF TRUNK
OR
FIBERGLASS BEFORE
ASSEMBLY

3/4 INCH SCREWS

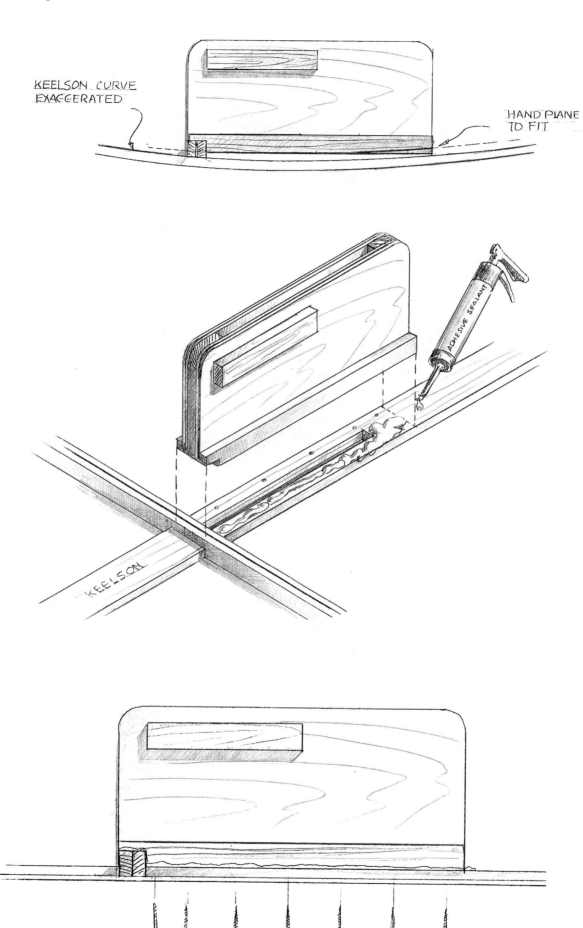

KEELSON CURVE
EXAGGERATED

HAND PLANE
TO FIT

ADHESIVE SEALANT

KEELSON

4. Center seat/dagger board trunk brace

Refer to the illustration for the layout of the center seat-brace which is constructed of 1" x 10" pine or fir. The seat is actually in two sections that are affixed to the cleats on the dagger board case, in the center of the boat, and to the seat risers at the sides. To strengthen the risers, fit 1 1/2" x 4" filler blocks between the risers and and the side and epoxy and screw these into place with 1 1/4" screws.

When the filler blocks are in, you can measure and cut the seats to fit between the sides of the hull and the dagger board case. When all fits properly, epoxy and screw the pieces into place with 1 1/4" stainless steel screws to both the risers and and filler blocks.

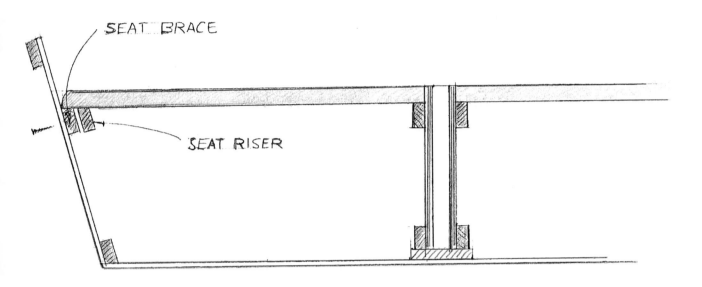

SEAT BRACE

SEAT RISER

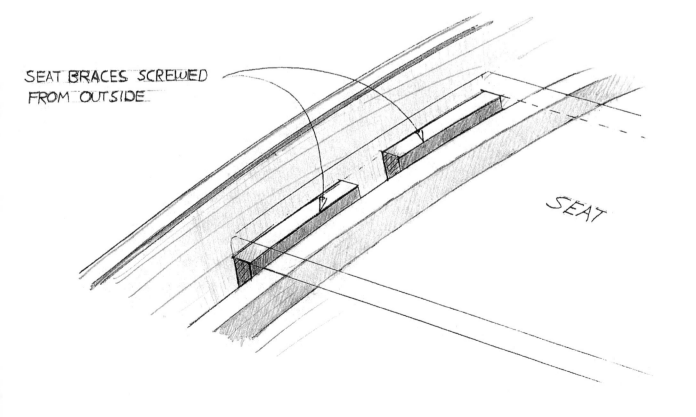

SEAT BRACES SCREWED FROM OUTSIDE

SEAT

5. Dagger board

The dagger board is constructed of 3/4" plywood of the dimensions indicated in the illustration. It should be coated with three coats of epoxy, sanding between each coat after the epoxy is no longer tacky.

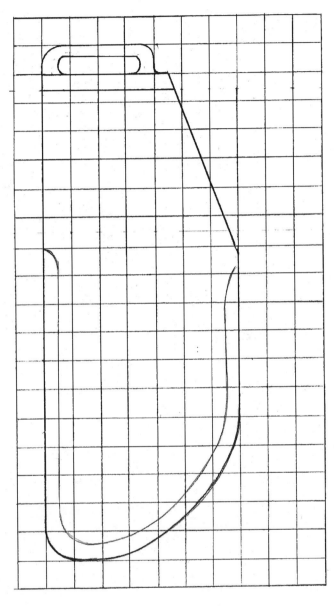

2" SQUARES

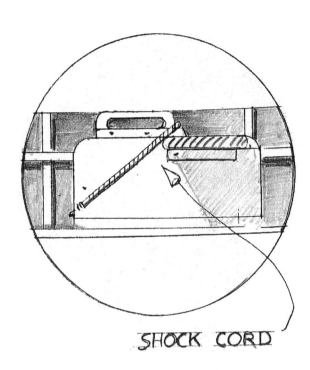

SHOCK CORD

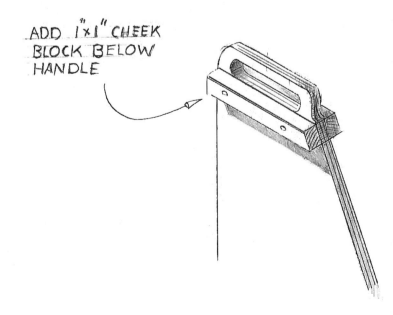

ADD 1"×1" CHEEK BLOCK BELOW HANDLE

6. Rudder and tiller

You can build a tiller out of a piece of 2" x 2" or laminate two pieces of 1" x 2". Taper to 1" x 1" at the forward end as indicated in the drawing. Two plywood "cheeks" glued to the end of the tiller allow you to attach it to the rudder with a stainless steel 3/8" diameter bolt and "jam" nut so it can raise and lower as if on a hinge.

The rudder is made of three pieces of 3/8" plywood: the center piece forms the rudder and the two side pieces or "cheeks" strengthen the assembly where it attaches to the transom. Refer to the illustration for dimensions and to see how to attach the "eye" bolts by drilling into the center rudder piece before epoxying the three pieces together.

The rudder is attached to the transom with eye bolts and the 1/4" brazing rod or you can use a 3/8" dowel. This arrangement will allow the rudder to "kick up" if it hits a submerged object.

Drill 1/4" holes and bolt two eye bolts to the transom along a vertical midline as indicated on the illustration. These eye bolts should match up with the eye bolts on the rudder.

Bend 1" of the brazing rod over to a right angle making an "L" shape at the end. Fit the rudder eye bolts to the transom eye bolts so the rudder eye bolts are on top and slide the rod through the eye bolts affixing the rudder to the transom. Or, if you prefer to use a dowel, cut the dowel to fit and attach a small knob or bead to the top as a stop and slide the dowel in place. (*See illustration on page* 62.)

2 INCH SQUARES

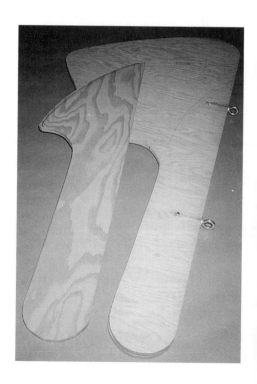

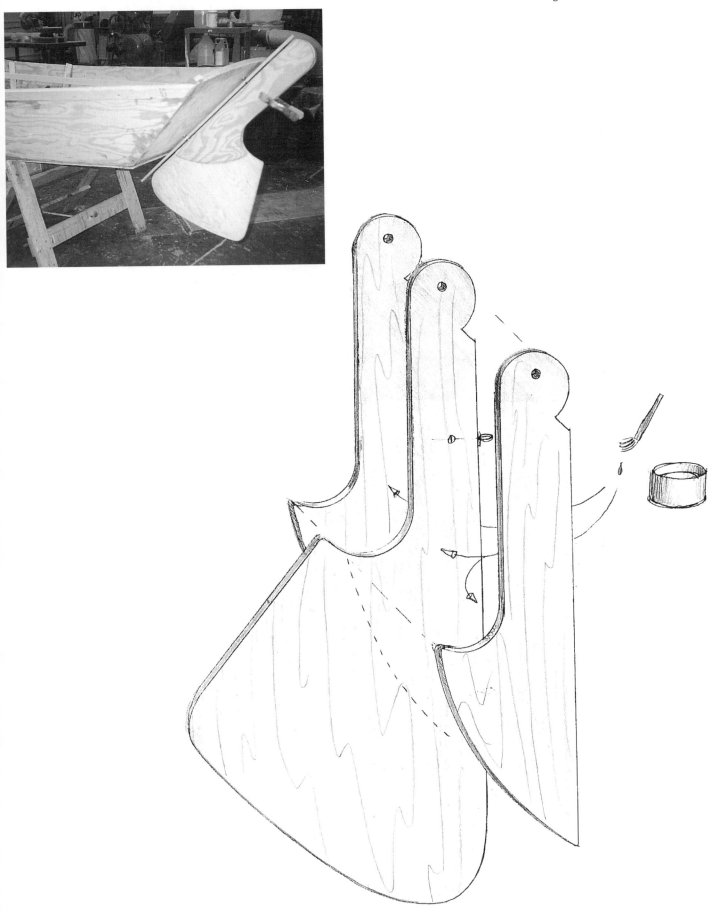

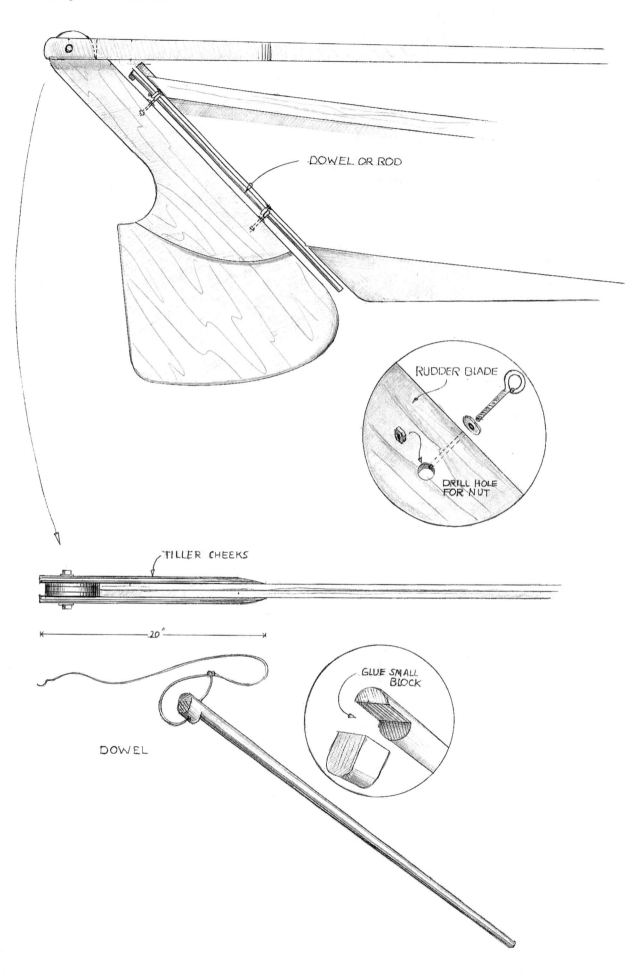

DOWEL OR ROD

RUDDER BLADE

DRILL HOLE
FOR NUT

TILLER CHEEKS

20"

GLUE SMALL
BLOCK

DOWEL

7. *Seat mast-brace (also called a mast "partner")*

The seat mast-brace is a seat with a hole in it so the mast can be stepped through it. Thus the seat functions as a brace for the mast. To add strength, the seat is fastened to the seat risers and to the sides with additional blocks as was the case with the center seat and you should install these 1 1/2" x 4" filler blocks first.

Fit a piece of 1" x 10" stock in position as indicated in the illustration. Attach this seat mast-brace to the seat risers with epoxy and three 1 1/4" screws at each end. Using a saber saw, carefully cut a 2 -3/4" square hole out of the center of the seat mast-brace. (Note: you'll need to drill a 3/8" starter hole in one corner so you can insert the saber saw blade.) It is through this hole that you will step the mast.

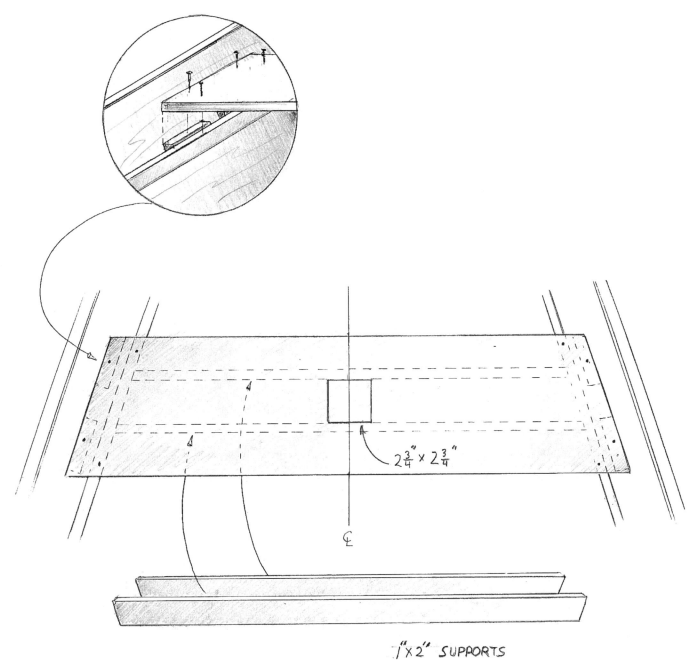

$2\frac{3}{4}"$ x $2\frac{3}{4}"$

1"X 2" SUPPORTS
GLUED AND SCREWED
UNDERNEATH

8. *Mast step*

The illustration shows the mast step location. The bottom of the mast will set into the mast step.

Mark out three 3 1/2" x 5" blocks in a piece of scrap 3/8" plywood. Clamp the plywood down, mark out and cut a 1 1/2" x 1 1/2" square hole out of the center of two of the blocks with your saber saw. Then cut the blocks out of the plywood. and laminate them together with epoxy and set aside until the epoxy cures.

After you build the mast, level the boat with a level laid across the gunwales. Set the mast step in place on the keelson directly under the hole in the seat-brace and step the mast to check for alignment. The mast should be plum (vertical) from side to side and rake slightly back (say 5°). Adjust the step accordingly and mark its position.

Bed the block in thickened epoxy and screw into place with four pre-drilled 2" stainless steel screws driven from the outside.

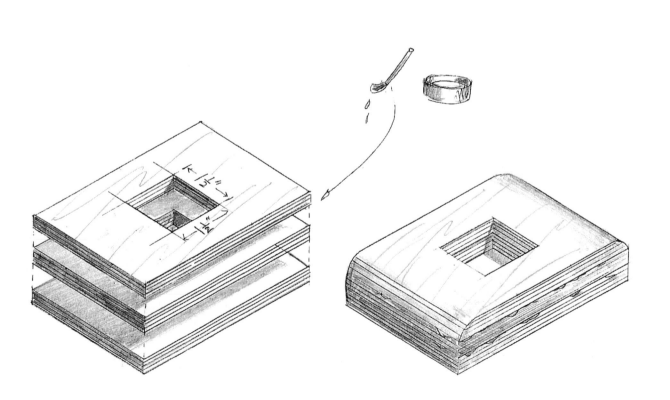

9. Mast

The mast is made by laminating two sections of 1 1/2" x 3" x 10' together as drawn. (These pieces can be gotten out of clear 2" x 4" stock that has been ripped to 1 1/2" x 3".)

Mix up enough epoxy to wet out the faces to be joined and then add thickened epoxy and clamp. The resulting "blank" is then planed to 2 1/2" x 2 1/2" at the seat mast-brace (9" from the lower end) and tapered to 2 1/4"at the bottom and 1 1/2" at the top. Then round off the edges. Fit the mast through the mast seat-brace (partner) to check for a snug fit and adjust if necessary.

Drill a 3/8" hole about 2" down from the top of the mast through which you will attach a block (pulley) to hoist the sail.

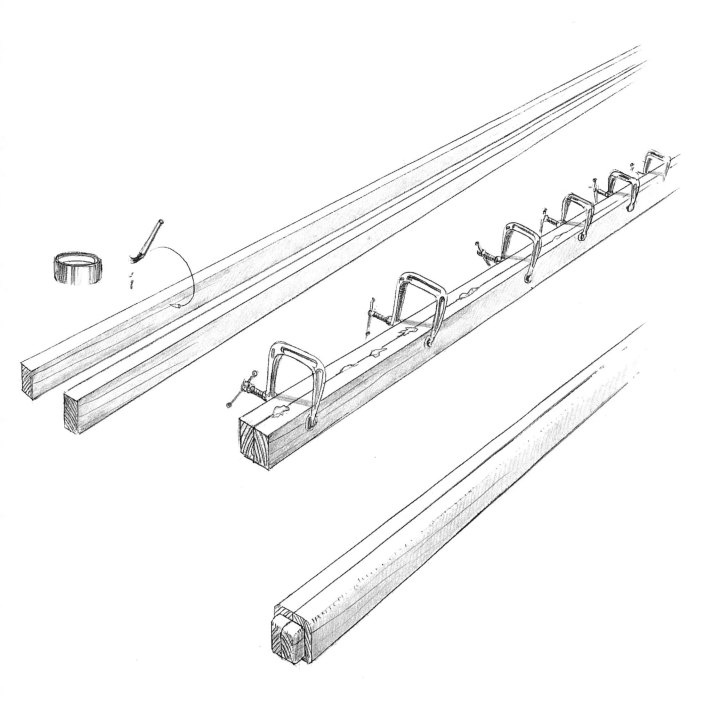

10. Gaff

The gaff supports the top of the sail. It is constructed out of clear 1 1/2" x 1 1/2" pine or fir.

Cut two pieces of 1" x 2" (actually 3/4" x 1 1/2") pine or fir 5' long. Laminate the two pieces together with epoxy to get a single 1 1/2" x 1 1/2" x 5' piece. With a plane, taper the gaff to 1" at each end and round the edges off. Drill a 1/4" hole at each end and a 3/8" hole 18" from one end.

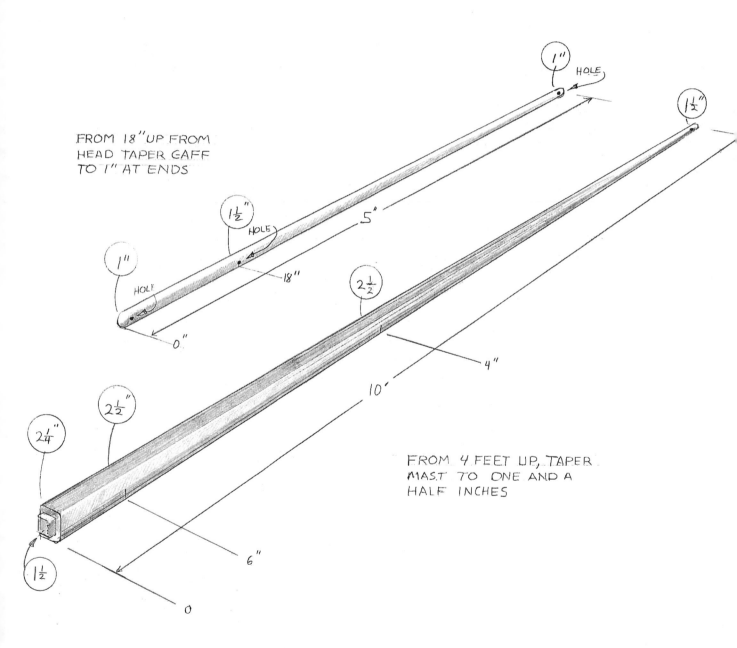

FROM 18" UP FROM HEAD TAPER GAFF TO 1" AT ENDS

FROM 4 FEET UP, TAPER MAST TO ONE AND A HALF INCHES

11. Skeg

Laminate two 4" x 48" pieces of your 3/8" plywood together with epoxy, clamping until cured. Cut the wedge shape as illustrated and fit this piece to the slight curve of the bottom. Glue it to the bottom as indicated with thickened epoxy and screw it from the inside with 2" # 10 stainless steel screws. Drive the screws, carefully into pre-drilled holes and don't over tighten as it is very easy to pull screws out of the end grain in plywood.

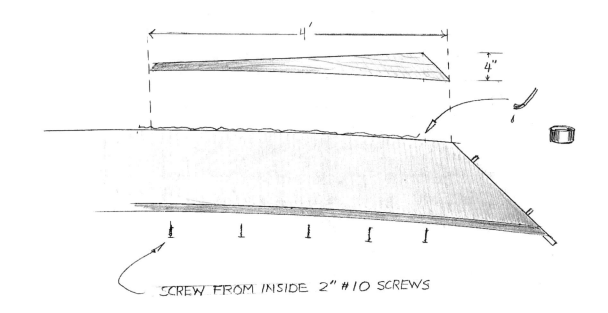

SCREW FROM INSIDE 2" #10 SCREWS

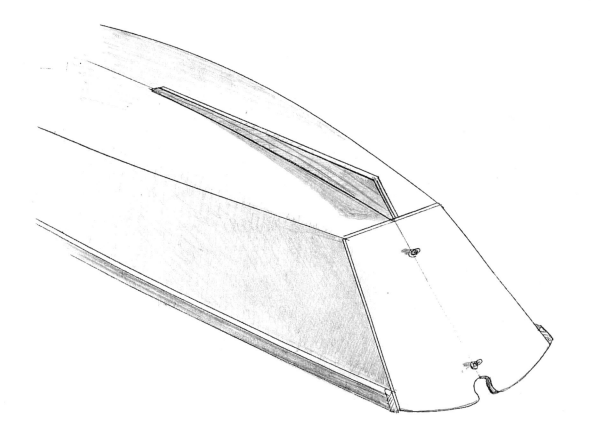

12. *Sails*

The drawing illustrates a simple sail plan. You can have the sail made up by any number of sail lofts. Check the ads in publications such as **Wooden**Boat magazine or look in your phone book for listing in your area.

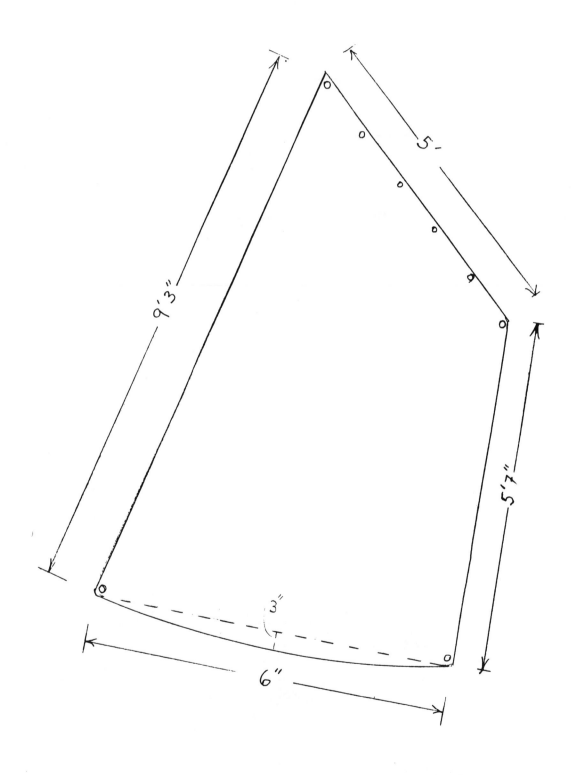

SECTION IV - SAFE USE

A. Intended use

When I think about using these skiffs I think about inland lakes, small coves and quiet rivers and streams. Their lightness makes them easy to cartop and drop into a body of water where there is no launch ramp. And their lines make them easy to row or drive with a small motor.

We use the boats in our aquatic ecology programs in which kids need to have access to stable boats for collecting activities. With one child at the oars and one or two pulling nets or collecting water samples, the boat functions very well. Their flat bottoms provide initial stability and make launching from a ramp or beach a simple operation.

As fishing boats they excel, again, because of their stability and because they are roomy with plenty of space for tackle boxes and other gear. At less than $ 200.00 a boat, the skiffs offer families an opportunity to get on the water without great financial sacrifice.

B. Safety equipment

Any boater must invest in Coast Guard approved personal flotation devices (PFD's) for each occupant of the boats. These can cost as little as $ 5.00 or 6.00 and are absolutely necessary and are required in many states. Also recommended is an anchor and enough line for the depths you will encounter, a bailing container and a signal light for night-time use.

For the outboard skiff, boaters should check local regulation concerning running lights and signaling devices. You may also need a class III throwable flotation device such as an approved boat cushion or life ring.

SECTION V : COMMUNITY BOAT BUILDING PROGRAMS

A. Building a successful program

In 1989, my colleagues Bill Bartoo, John Montague and I, having founded the Center for Watercraft Studies at the State University College at Buffalo, attended the Traditional Small Craft Association's annual small craft workshop at the Mystic Seaport in Mystic, Connecticut. Held on the first week-end in June, this event features workshops and talks, but the real attraction of the event is the scores of boats that are in the water. Some are museum boats while others are brought by participants on the condition that they be made available for other participants to try out.

Picture such a gathering of devotees of fine small craft on a sunny Saturday in June on a historic waterfront when, out of the mist, come several pulling boats driven by grunting, chanting teenagers. All eyes turn to these kids as they beach their boats and swagger ashore —- right into the midst of the activities.

Those of us who sauntered over (boat people always "saunter" when about to inspect a new arrival on the waterfront), were rewarded with stories of how these kids built their boats as part of a summer youth program in Hartford, Connecticut and how they used them in rowing races on the Connecticut River and elsewhere. Pride evident, these kids were really turned on.

Throughout the day the kids participated in activities, often assisting the older participants in launching and getting under way. They tried out all the boats, casting knowledgeable eyes on the details of construction and craftsmanship. Courteous and helpful, they were a positive addition to the event and fun to watch.

It was later in the day, when Ed Flanagan, their mentor, talked about the program that the kids were in

and about their backgrounds, describing the poverty and problems these kids came from. Yet, here, in this most cultured of settings, the kids fit right in. Something was going on here.

The next morning we grabbed Ed, went to breakfast and learned all we could about how he did what he did to change these lives in so significant a way.

And we came back to Buffalo convinced that we had a found a direction to pursue in our own community. It was a direction that built on what we had begun to observe in our own programs.

In our boat building classes at the college, we had witnessed the self-confidence building potential of boat building. I've worked in arts education all my professional life and have seen the power of the arts to change young lives. But, in the case of the plastic arts (drawing, painting, ceramics, etc.), these changes occur on an individual level. In the case of boat building the changes occur both on an individual level as a student learns new skills, but also on a group or team level as kids work together to produce big objects that are going to lift them on the water and transport them over it. There is an almost magical power in what boats can do for kids. And, unlike any experience I had had before, there are many adults in the boating community who are willing to help.

Inspired by Flanagan's experience we began to offer boat building workshops to teachers and young students in the public schools, learning as we went. At first we built some kayaks with a group of technology teachers to involve them in the process. But the kayaks were too time consuming to keep kids' attention and awfully expensive to build. Then we tried some dinghies built from Clark-Craft kits and that worked pretty well because it produced quicker results.

The real breakthrough came when Mike O'Brien, Senior Editor at **WoodenBoat Magazine**, suggested a design which we adapted and named The Six-Hour Canoe. Built of two sheets of plywood and a few pieces of dimensional lumber, the canoe could be put together, painted and launched in less than twenty hours. Even more important, for keeping the kids' interest, it looked like a boat within three hours. Painted with exterior house paint it offered an inexpensive vehicle around which to build a program for inner-city kids.

It was perfect! Over the ensuing years we have built hundreds of the boats and through our book, **Building the Six-Hour Canoe**, thousands more have been built around the world. Having the right vehicle enabled us, here in Buffalo, to introduce kids in city school and community programs to the magic of boat building. It enabled us to provide an opportunity for quality interaction between adults and children That built self-esteem and produced a lasting product.

The format involves three week-ends of work and a forth of launch festivities including the use of the boats in an aquatic ecology experience. In the next section we'll get into the specifics of the program.

B. Mentored boat building: a sample program

Early on we learned that some things work and some don't. What follows is an outline of a successful four week, mentored boat building for junior high school kids.

Why pick junior high school kids? I had always heard that this age group is hard to control, unfocused, etc. Our experience has been quite different. This age group is highly capable of learning woodworking skills, is direct able, and hasn't discovered the opposite sex to any great degree. In fact, they are a delight to deal with if you make the necessary preparations. They are:

- find cooperating agencies to provide the kids, but make sure you set the rules. We work with the public schools, Children's Hospital of Buffalo, Boys and Girls Clubs, foster care providers and social service agencies to name a few. Just make sure that your partners understand the parameters and that they are truly committed to the project,
- secure your funding. The skiff costs about $ 250.00 for materials. We charge $ 350.00 to cover overhead, refreshments, etc. It isn't hard to get sponsors for one boat,
- secure your workspace. We have a large shop, but we've worked outside (exhausting) and under a large tent (nice). You need about 200 square feet per team.

- start cautiously. We operate our most successful programs with only eight kids. But this means eight mentors and eight parents/guardians for a total of at least twenty-four people. That's enough if you want to avoid chaos. John and I have built 25 boats with 50 kids at one time - but that's not a high quality experience.
- involve adults. We use older teenage and adult mentors, preferably from classes here at the college so the kids have somebody to relate to. It works best if you have one mentor for each kid,
- parents. In our most successful week-end programs we insist that at least one parent/guardian of family member work with the child and mentor. In many cases this is the first time parents and kids have worked together and the results are powerful. For a child who has been swept aside by busy or inept parents, a few week-ends in which that child is the sole focus of the parent is good medicine, indeed,
- design a permission/release/commitment form that commits the kids and parent to full participation. Don't allow people to come and go as they please. You want them there full-time or they'll fall hopelessly behind. That said, it is your job to make sure that no kid fails if he or she tries,
- train your mentors to insure that the kids, not the adults build the boat. They are capable of sawing, drilling, driving screws, planing, etc. Just provide basic instruction and a guiding hand. It can be of great benefit for a parent to observe that his or her kid has these capabilities.
- plan well and have all tools and materials ready to go when the kids arrive. Nothing kills momentum like standing around. We pre-cut all parts so the kids are just assembling. This also eliminates the use of stationary power tools and extreme liability,
- build in intensity. As you'll see when you get to the section on scheduling, we push the kids pretty hard. In fact. with both the Six Hour Canoe and the Week-end Skiff, we prepare a "kit" of pre-cut part so the kids can get the boat up by lunchtime of the first day. Once they actually see what they're going to get we usually have to drag them away from their work for lunch and clean-up at the end of the day,
- take pictures and show them around the next week. Kids like to see themselves,
- plan a gala launch and invite the families to bring favorite foods and celebrate what their children have accomplished,
- pick a safe place to launch the boats and don't over-instruct. Let the kids discover how to maneuver their boats. Have safety boats in the water to assist them but don't impose and *always make sure all participants wear a* PFD *whenever on the water*,
- once the kids are comfortable with their boats have them play follow the leader, run obstacle courses, relays, etc.
- offer the opportunity to participate in a Coast Guard safe boating course such as Make Sure - Make Shore.

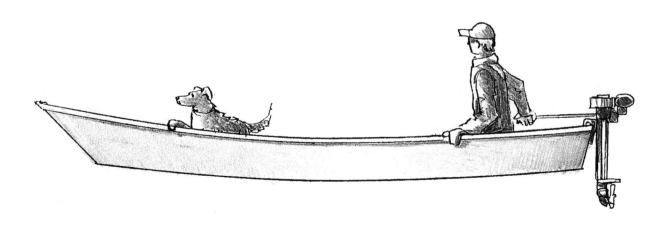

C. Sample schedule

1. *Preparation*

The kits that we prepare are designed to eliminate down-time. In an intensive, 20 hour program there isn't time to wait for epoxy to cure on basic components such as hull panel butt blocks and frames. And, with prepared pieces, we avoid the need for the participants to use heavy power equipment or to stand around while we mill out parts. So, the following should be ready when the participants walk in the door:

- hull side panels cut out, planed and butt- blocked,
- positions of frames and half frames marked on the side panels,
- stems cut out and glued together,
- frames cut out, glued together, and angles planed,
- transom cut out, battens glued on and angles planed,
- chine logs ripped with bevels,
- gunwales and seat risers ripped.

These parts can be bundled or laid out in stations along with:
- a pair of horses,
- a can of 1" drywall screws,
- a can of 1"ring nails,
- a cordless drill with bits and Phillips head bits,
- a low angle block plane,
- 2 hammers,
- 6 spring clamps,
- 2 C-clamps,
- a 2" x 4" x 4' sanding board with # 50 sandpaper,
- safety glasses for each participant.

At a central <u>glue</u> station you should have:
- epoxy in large containers with pumps,
- a container of wood flour,
- acid brushes for applying the epoxy,
- 4 - 6 ounce paper cups for epoxy,
- disposable rubber or vinyl gloves.

At a central <u>tool</u> station have:
- tape measures,
- T-bevels,
- combination squares,
- lots of pencils,
- hand saws,
- a saber saw,
- pieces of 2" x 4" block to use as sanding blocks,
- sanders and sandpaper.

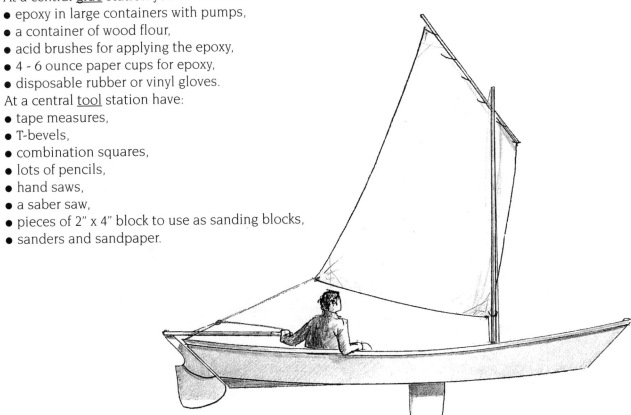

2. *Construction schedule*

Day 1 (Saturday: 9:00 - 4:00): beginning on the first day the participants will follow the sequence as outlined in this manual in **Part II: Hull Assembly**.
- By late morning all boats should have their frames, half-frames, stems and transoms glued in.
- After lunch, install and plane the chine logs and glue on the bottom.
- Before leaving for the day install the gunwales and seat risers.

Day 2 (Sunday: 1:00 - 5:00)
- Remove all drywall screws and sink all nails flush with the surface.
- Plane the bottom edges, round off frames ends and trim the stem and plane the stem edge and sheer line.
- Block sand the entire boat.
- Cut and fit the seats.
- Varnish the gunwales

Day 3 (Saturday: 9:00 - 12:00)
- Remove the seats and risers.
- Finish sand the boat with # 120 sandpaper.
- Mask off the gunwales with masking tape.
- Varnish the seats and risers.
- Prime the surface of the hull.

Day 4 (Saturday 9:00 - 12:00)
- Paint inside of the boat.
- Install the risers and seats.
- Turn the boat over and paint the outside.

D. Alternative Schedules

The schedule in the previous section gets the job done in four week-ends. You can build the boats in evening or after-school sessions, but should add at least five hours to your schedule because of the inefficiency of shorter, more frequent meetings when much time is lost for setting up and cleaning up operations. Sea Fever runs after-school programs and finds that what takes twenty hours in the week-end program can take much longer in other formats.

Another interesting approach is to build the boats in one week-end and then take them to participating schools or community programs where the kids can involve their classmates and friends in sanding and painting the boats. This is very productive because the kids really like the time to do complex paint schemes and the more intense program doesn't allow for that.

E. Environmental education

One of the advantages for us of being affiliated with a major college and university system is the interdisciplinary opportunities that present themselves. For example, our college has a major research center known as the Great Lakes Center for Environmental Research and Education. Several years ago we began to collaborate with GLC because the center uses boats of all sizes for research and we had access to boats of all sizes. As time went on it became evident that our small boats and boat building programs for kids could become vehicles by which the Great Lakes Center could develop environmental education programs for the public schools and community.

The collaboration evolved when I was invited by the director, Dr. Stephen Brandt, to become an associate director for community outreach and service and was asked to explore and develop community-based environmental programs using the center's faculty and graduate students as resources.

In exploring resources I became aware of some exciting water quality monitoring materials for young people and we decided that a great way to interest kids in aquatic ecology might be to combine boat building with water quality monitoring activities. So, a group of graduate students headed by Mike Weimer, developed a series of activities that could become part of our launch day program.

Launch day was in late April that year and spring was very late - in fact, the canal was choked in ice and we considered postponing. But everything was set and we had enough safety boats and personnel so we went ahead. The result was an exciting day in which the kids dodged and paddled around ice chunks that drifted back and forth as the wind direction changed. We even had to "rescue" one boater who got locked in a pack of ice in a wind shift.

For the aquatic ecology part of the day, the graduate students had prepared a great list of activities. For example:

- they gave short talks with special demonstrations on the region's geography, geology, social history, water chemistry, effects of pollution and the food web to place the collecting activities in perspective,

- they took the participants and their families on a tour of the field station with its labs and "critter" holding tanks, explaining the research activities that were going on,

- Mike designed a manual that the kids could use to enter data from readings and observations that they took on the water and on the shore. It also contained drawings of typical specimens they would encounter and many of the kids took the manuals into their schools to show their teachers and classmates,

- the graduate students took the kids out in center boats for some field collecting and the kids used their own boats for others,

- back in the field station lab, (about fifty feet from the water), the graduate students and the kids inspected the water and bottom samples in trays and under microscopes, cataloging the "critters" and plants they found ranging from fish to plankton and even a mud puppy that kept jumping out of the tray and running down the hall.

The new program was a bit rough around the edges but its effects on the participants was fantastic. At times we could not contain their excitement and sense of discovery. And this held true for the parents as well.

We conducted subsequent programs for groups ranging from inner city children from impoverished circumstances to more fortunate kids from a Montessori school. And the stories began to come back to us. One child had been suicidal (unknown to us) - feeling abandoned in a family that was dealing with the catastrophic health concerns of a sibling. Working with his parents who were focused on him alone was powerful medicine and his entire disposition changed for the better as did his grades in school. In another case a girl had been diagnosed as having Attention Deficit Disorder. But in the workshops it was observed by her counselor that the real problem was a neurotic parent, which led to a change in the way the family was treated at the clinic. And, a young boy, who had very little self-motivation, got so turned on that he joined an after-school rowing program. There were many more.

During the next year a professor of earth science, Stephen Vermette, developed a menu driven water quality testing mini-curriculum that he named "*The Aquanaut*" and we began to use that very effective approach to strengthen the aquatic ecology part of our program. Now offered in teacher training workshops, the **Aquanaut** consists of an illustrated manual and a kit of equipment and chemicals that enables teachers and environmental educators to conduct meaningful field exercises in local waters. These exercises produce data that can be used evaluate the health of the waters in question and introduces kids to the excitement of conducting serious science in the field. And some of the tests and sampling collecting can be done from a skiff like the one detailed in this manual.Dr. Vermette is planning to publish the **Aquanaut** so it can be made available for dissemination. He can be reached at: The Department of Earth Science and Science Education, Buffalo State College, 1300 Elmwood Ave., Buffalo, NY, 14222.

In conclusion I would have to say that there was some reservation about opening the lab to a group of junior high school kids. This is a serious research facility and the graduate students, while willing, seemed a bit anxious about the outcome. However, the clear success of the program and the effect it had on the children was so compelling that we have had willing volunteers for every subsequent group. And, a few days ago, one of our post-doctoral fellows asked me when the kids were coming back. I knew we had arrived.

APPENDIX

Sources of Supplies

Some materials are not available at local building suppliers in many locales. Here are some suggestions with which we are familiar. For a more comprehensive listing, pick up a copy of WoodenBoat magazine at the newsstand.

marine plywood
Boulter Plywood Corp.
24 Broadway
Sommerville, MA 02145
617-666-1340

Harbor Sales
1401 Russell St.
Baltimore, MD 21230
1-800-345-1712

marine fastenings and epoxy supplies
Clark Craft
16 Aqua Lane
Tonawanda, NY 14150
716-873-2640

WEST epoxy and pumps
Gugeon Bros., Inc.
P.O. Box 908
Bay City, MI 48707
517-684-7286

Pre-cut Parts and Boats

For those builders who do not have access to a bandsaw, we can make a stem and four frame gussets and mail them to you. We also build these boats to any degree of finish. For a price list write to Dick Butz at 189 Union Street, Hamburg, NY 14075 or call 716-649-8018.

Join An Organization

Once you build your boat you may want some friends to go boating with or to give you advice and moral support. Here's a great organization that has many local chapters and it only costs $ 15.00/year to join.

Traditional Small Craft Association
P.O. Box 350
Mystic, CT 06355

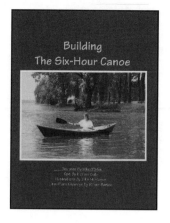

BUILDING THE SIX-HOUR CANOE

BY MIKE O'BRIEN AND RICHARD BUTZ

ILLUSTRATIONS BY JOHN MONTAGUE • LINE DRAWINGS BY WILLIAM BARTOO

Quickly and simply built, the Six-Hour Canoe is suitable for builders and paddlers young and old — a wonderful way to get afloat. This book contains scale plans, specifications, a tool list, step-by-step instructions. All building operations are illustrated with sketches and photographs. The canoe is constructed from a single 4'x16' sheet of marine plywood and a few pieces of dimensional lumber and, with epoxy glued seams, is watertight from the moment it hits the water. When completed, the canoe is 15'3" in length with a 31½" beam. 8½"x11", softcover, 64 pgs. many photos & drawings.

"It's a great how-to, a great read and probably will get as many folks into the wonderful world of modest watercraft as the popular 'Instant Boat' series. . . . it is easy to build, cheap, a great learning and teaching took and surely something that will help a lot of people get started in the boat hobby." **Messing About in BOATS**

BUILDING SWEET DREAM

AN ULTRALIGHT SOLO CANOE FOR SINGLE & DOUBLE PADDLE

BY MARC PETTINGILL

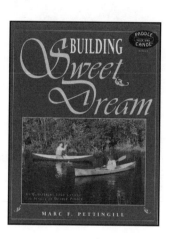

Building Sweet Dream is a complete how-to manual covering all phases of building and finishing. It includes dimensioned hull plans, detailed building sequence heavily illustrated with step-by-step photographs, tips and techniques for painting and varnishing, and hard-to-find background and reference material. **Sweet Dream** is easily and quickly built using hand and basic electric tools, by one person in a one-car garage or small workshop. Using "folded plywood" techniques shown in this book, build a 12', 13' or 14' 28-lb. arc-bottom hull canoe. 8½"x11", softcover, 176 pgs. illus.

"Usually boats designed for simple building are rather uninspiring to look at. Not the Sweet Dream. . . . .one of the loveliest canoes to come out of a backyard. . . . There are ample photographs and diagrams, and the instructional text is clear and un-ambiguous." **International Marine Boating Books Catalog, 1996**

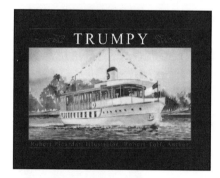

TRUMPY

BY ROBERT TOLF • ILLUSTRATED BY ROBERT PICARDAT

In **Trumpy**, author Robert Tolf traces the Trumpy family from its origins through emigration to the United States. John Trumpy has earned his place in yachting history by creating elegant and well-built yachts of enduring beauty, including fine motoryachts, classic houseboats, U.S. government boats and sailing vessels. **Trumpy** is richly illustrated by marine artist Robert Picardat. Included are some original Trumpy plans, a complete list of all Trumpy yachts built and those known to survive. 11"x8½", hardcover, 224 pgs, 32 color illus. *"To honor the Trumpy legacy, Tiller Publishing of St. Michaels, MD, has produced its own masterpiece. . . . (Buy two books and cut one up for framing!)"* **Chesapeake Bay Magazine**

SPECIAL OFFER: TRUMPY ART PRINT. Featuring 25 of the exquisite full-color paintings and drawings from **Trumpy**. The deep blue background and rich gold type highlight Robert Picardat's stunning renderings of such elegant Trumpy yachts as **Sequoia II,** the Presidential Yacht from 1933-1977. Printed on high quality paper. Approximate size: 22" x 34". **Limited Quantity!**

COMING SOON FROM TILLER

OF YACHTS AND MEN BY WILLIAM ATKIN. The famed boat designer's warm, entertaining and informative reminiscences of a lifetime enjoying boats. In his own words, it is *"an account of many happy years of building, designing and living with small boats; with plans and illustrations of some of these boats, and the circumstances under which they were conceived."*

BOATS BY PURDY BY ALAN DINN. The story of the Purdy Boat Company of Port Washington, NY, and two unforgettable perfectionists, Ned & Gil Purdy, who contributed greatly to a boatbuilding era filled with excitement, hope, and pride in workmanship and individual accomplishments. Many illustrations and photos, Purdy boat plans and a complete list of Purdy boats built and extant.

CRUISING SAILBOAT KINETICS: *THE ART, SCIENCE & MAGIC OF CRUISING BOAT DESIGN.* Danny Greene's classic about boat design, written for the everyday, non-professional sailor, demystifies boat design terminology and concepts. It opens up for recreational sailors a new world of understanding why sailboats act the way they do. Includes plans of some of the best yacht designs of the last twenty years.   ***AND MANY MORE . . .***

PRACTICAL JUNK RIG

DESIGN AERODYNAMICS AND HANDLING
BY HG HASLER AND JK McLEOD

In this encyclopedic volume the late "Blondie" Hasler and his partner Jock McLeod have synthesized 25 years of research and development of the junk rig as adapted to western craft. into the foremost major work on the fore-and-aft Chinese junk rig. **Practical Junk Rig** examines the design and aerodynamic theory behind junk rigs and discusses how bet to sail them. It is not a historical treatise but rather a detailed analysis of the intricacies of the rig, accessible to both amateur owners and professional designers. It examines the rig in detail, the principles that underlie it, considers alternative shapes and arrangements and performance. 9¼" x11¼", hardcover, 244 pgs., color & b&w photos, tables & detailed drawings. *"There is no better or more comprehensive work on the subject available . . . it should be considered THE handbook on junk rigs for anyone interested in the subject."* **Sailing**

SEAWORTHINESS

THE FORGOTTEN FACTOR BY C.A. MARCHAJ

Newly updated and revised, this book is a highly readable critical analysis of how the search for racing yacht performance has led to the development of sailing yachts with potentially dangerous seakeeping characteristics. Based upon the highest degree of practical and academic research, it demonstrates how modern yacht design often sacrifices safety for speed and for other considerations, and it maintains that dramatic changes in design philosophy are needed to prevent further loss of life at sea. This is a major work which will help change the thinking on popular design trends for both racing and cruising yachts. 7½"x10½"m hardcover, 384 pgs. with 140 line drawings and 50 photos.
"For the first time we are offered logical scientific criteria which help us to assess the likely seaworthiness of one boat or another. That is the great advance displayed in this book." **Practical Boat Owner**

STEEL BOATBUILDING

FROM PLANS TO LAUNCHING BY THOMAS E. COLVIN

STEEL BOATBUILDING combines both volumes of Tom Colvin's masterwork on building boats from steel in one complete volume. This book offers an overall view of the subject from raw materials to the finished vessel. The wealth of detail pertinent to every step in the building, fitting out, and launching of a 25- to 79-foot yacht or commercial vessel will ease the first-time builder or the professional over problems that might otherwise have seemed insurmountable. Part 1 covers the building of hull and decks, while Part 2 takes you through the remainder of the process, including joinery, machinery installation, rigging, and launching. 7"x10", softcover, 480 pgs., many illus. *"There is probably no one more uniquely qualified to pen the ultimate book on steel boatbuilding than author, designer, builder and live-aboard cruising man Tom Colvin."* **Cruising World** • *"It's the best I've seen on starting from square one and getting through a completed hull. . . Colvin's book provides a reasonable substitute, both in terms of understanding the magnitude of the task and how to accomplish it."* **The Houston Post**

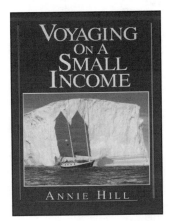

VOYAGING ON A SMALL INCOME

BY ANNIE HILL

Annie and Peter Hill voyage on **Badger**, a Benford 34' Sailing Dory. An income of £1,300 per year lets them do this without worrying about stopping to work. They built **Badger** a decade ago, live aboard her, and have sailed her over 60,000 miles. Annie wrote this book to answer all the questions about what they're doing. If you want to follow their wake or set off on your own adventures, there's a wealth of practical information on how-to-do-it here. 8½"x11", softcover, 192 pgs, photos, illustrations & drawings. Includes the Benford plywood and epoxy dory designs like the Hill's **Badger** and many variations from 26' to 37½'. *"This book leaps into the 'must read' category for anyone contemplating living aboard and getting about, whether on a small or large income, and the 'should read' category for all cruising people."* **Yachting World** • *"The best book we've read to date on liveaboard cruising."* **Messing About in BOATS**

> LOOK FOR THE FURTHER ADVENTURES OF BADGER & HER CREW IN ANNIE HILL'S NEW BOOK MANGOES & MUTTON COMING IN 1997 FROM TILLER

SMALL CRAFT PLANS

BENFORD DESIGN GROUP

15 sets of plans for open boats, skiffs and tenders, from 7' to 18'. 8½"x11", softcover, 96 pgs., illus.

"Let's get it straight up front: . . . Benford knows that readers will build directly from the book . . . In fact, he encourages the process by including full working drawings and tables of offsets for all of the designs."   **WoodenBoat**

POCKET CRUISERS & TABLOID YACHTS, VOLUME 1

REVISED EDITION

BENFORD DESIGN GROUP

Complete building plans for several small cruis boats, including 14' and 20' Tug Yachts, 17' and 25' F tail Steam Launches, a 14' offshore cruising sloop and Catboat. Newly revised edition 1996. 8½"x11", softcov 96 pgs., illus.

"All of the plans exhibit the professional presentation well-conceived accommodations typical of the author's work   **WoodenB**

SMALL SHIPS, 4TH EDITION

BENFORD DESIGN GROUP

The latest volume of ideas from 'The Liveaboard Specialists,' it contains scores of detailed study plans of tugs, freighters, ferries, excursion boats, trawler yachts, houseboats and fishing vessels. 8½"x11", softcover, 304 pgs., color and b&w photos.

"I have spent **hours** *perusing* **Small Ships** *to my utter delight. Here is Benford at his best . . . original, fun, and thought provoking, which is what makes this book worth owning, not just reading. It is a book which will be referred to again and again."*   **Coastal Cruising**

CRUISING DESIGNS, 4TH EDITION

BENFORD DESIGN GRO

A catalog of plans for great cruising boats, sail power for living aboard. The fourth edition include number of designs new since the third edition. 8½"x1 softcover, 96 pgs, heavily illustrated with photos and drawings.

*"****Cruising Designs*** *is highly recommended, but if read in conjunction with* **Voyaging On A Small Income** *I fear for you. The authors should put a disclaimer on the co absolving themselves from responsibility should the rea decide to chuck their day job, get the boat, purchase a big st of Admiralty charts and leave on the next tide. In fact, com think of it that sounds a good idea . . ."*   **Classic B**

TILLER PUBLISHING • P.O. BOX 445 • ST. MICHAELS, MD 21663 • CREDIT CARD ORDER LINE **1-800-6TILLER**